ECO
fresh
BIO
Natural
FOOD
ORGANIC
local
bio
100%
fresh
local
food
local
farm
FARM
BIO
NATURAL
ECO
fresh
bio
BIO
local
BIO
farm
product
Natural
Green
FOOD
ORGANIC
local
bio
100%
fresh
local
food
local
farm
FARM
BIO
NATURAL

A FARMGIRL'S TABLE

JESSICA ROBINSON

GIBBS SMITH
TO ENRICH AND INSPIRE HUMANKIND

First Edition
17 18 19 20 21 5 4 3 2 1

Published by
Gibbs Smith
P.O. Box 667
Layton, Utah 84041

1.800.835.4993 orders
www.gibbs-smith.com

Designed by Rita Sowins/Sowins Design
Printed and bound in Hong Kong

Gibbs Smith books are printed on either recycled, 100% post-consumer waste, FSC-certified papers or on paper produced from sustainable PEFC-certified forest/controlled wood source. Learn more at www.pefc.org.

Library of Congress Cataloging-in-Publication Data
Names: Robinson, Jessica (Event planner), author.
Title: A farmgirl's table / Jessica Robinson.
Description: First edition. | Layton, Utah : Gibbs Smith, [2017] |
Includes index.
Identifiers: LCCN 2016031628 | ISBN 9781423642183 (jacketless hardcover)
Subjects: LCSH: Cooking, American. | Farm life--United States. | Farm produce--United States. | LCGFT: Cookbooks.
Classification: LCC TX715 .R6535 2017 | DDC 641.5973--dc23
LC record available at https://lccn.loc.gov/2016031628

TO MY PARENTS. IF IT WERE NOT FOR THE RURAL UPBRINGING THEY PROVIDED, I WOULD NOT BE WHERE I AM TODAY.

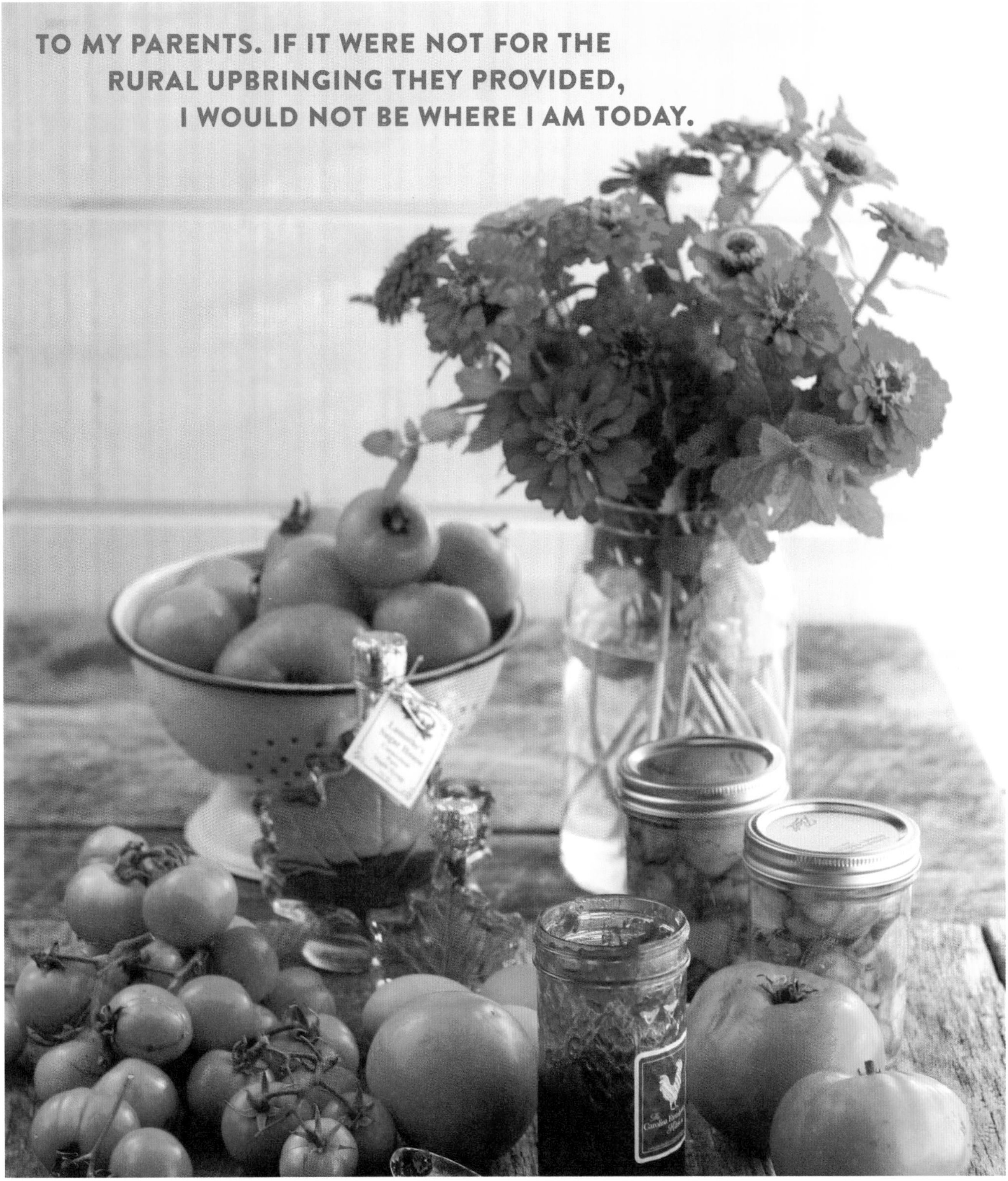

MARKET PANTRY
UNSALTED
BUTTER
SWEET CREAM

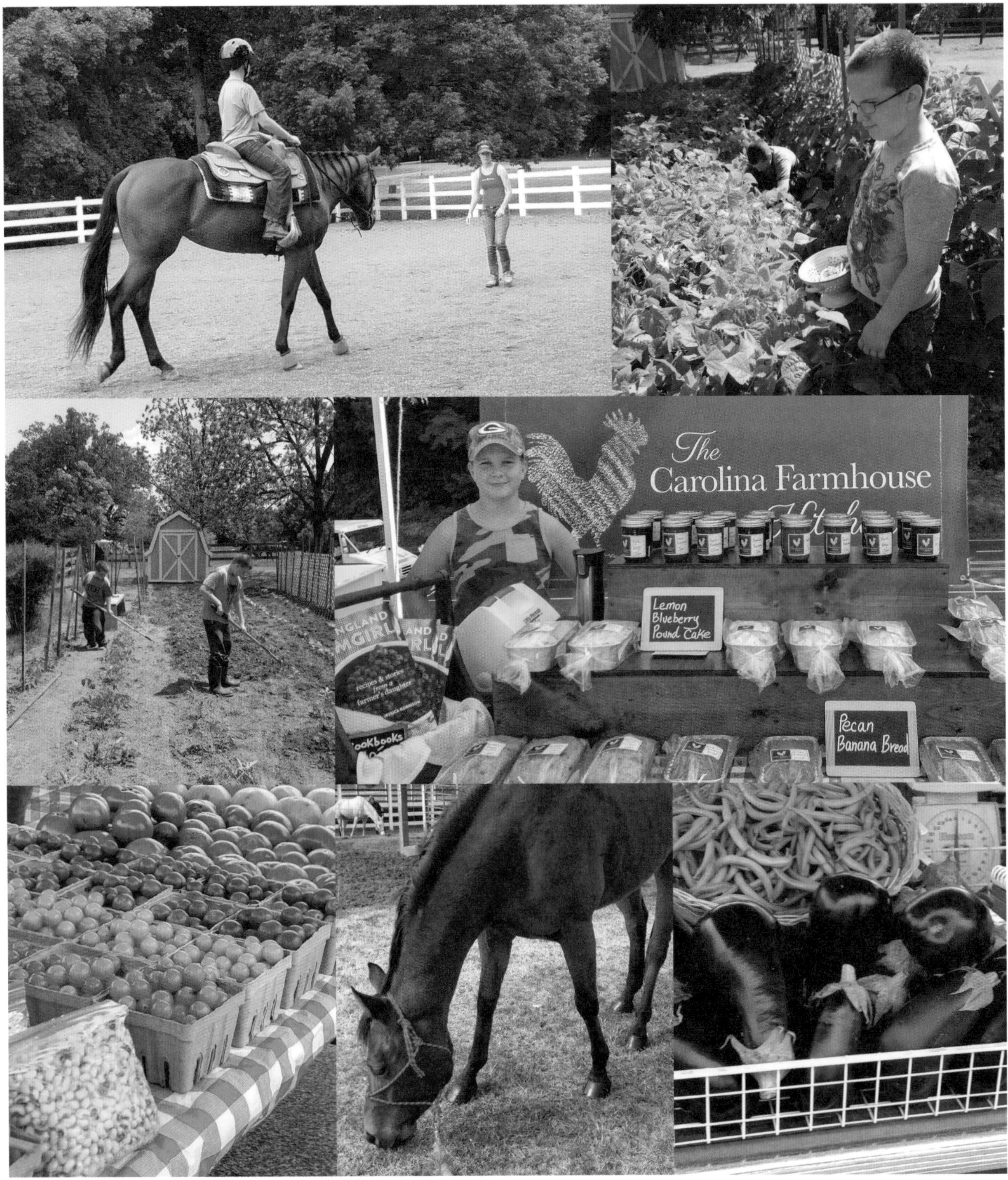
The
Carolina Farmhouse
Lemon
Blueberry
Pound Cake
Pecan
Banana Bread
recipes & stories
from a
farmer's daughter

NOT EVERYONE IS FORTUNATE ENOUGH TO GROW UP ON A FARM, BUT EVERYONE CAN COOK AS IF THEY DID. My cookbook was forged for anyone who has the spirit of farm-fresh cooking inside them. It's for moms and dads who incorporate heirloom tomatoes into the flower garden, and it's for the home bakers who are always looking for the perfect baking pan to complete their collection. It's for the suburban farmer with an oversized plot of land she cultivates and the urbanite who simply grows a few tomatoes and a bit of basil on his back patio. Even if you're not blessed with a green thumb, these recipes will inspire you to seek out the freshest ingredients at farmers markets and vegetable stands. Entice your family and friends with the savory aromas of homemade Boeuf Bourguignon (page 96) and homemade Potato Rolls (page 119). Or serve a special breakfast of easy-to-make Farmer's Quiche (page 19) and Spiced Apple Jam (page 71).

This book will help you cook your way through each season and celebration with confidence. I'll share some of my tips with you, including ones for planning an outdoor summer barbeque that's easy and fun (see page 50). I learned through running a floral design company for over seventeen years that it's all in the details. Just a few touches can add to the enjoyment of a meal by offering a beautiful environment. Gathering loose blooms, herbs, and berries from your garden or utilizing seasonal fruits and vegetables adds texture to your backyard soirées while preserving a feeling of simplicity.

I'm an old-fashioned farm-taught home cook who learned how to make almost everything from scratch. My talented parents taught me how to make fruit roll-ups, sauces, jams, pastries, cakes, candies, and confections. On an average day, you'll find me with my strawberry-blonde hair pulled through a pink camouflage ball cap and work boots laced up, working in the garden, canning up a batch of jam, or riding my horse, Lola.

This life is the life I was born to and adore. I grew up on a small Connecticut farm where my parents raised hogs and produced pure maple syrup and other confections. I still remember the sweet, sugary-smelling steam that escaped from the sugarhouse cupola doors as we processed sap. The beautiful end result was bottle after bottle of amber syrup that lined the windowsill. When my parents added a commercial kitchen, my mother crafted custom wedding cakes along with other maple confections. That kitchen became my farmgirl playground, where I developed many of the recipes in this book. I have fond memories of meals my parents and I shared around a worn butcher-block table in the sugarhouse during sugaring season, when my dad would work late into the night boiling sap. I hope my book will help you build warm family memories too.

My family had a whirlwind arrival in North Carolina after my husband got a new job. To tell you the truth, we jumped first and thought about it later. After three years, I've never had a moment's regret. I've made incredible friends who have become family. People take care of one another in the rural farming community where I live, much in the same way that my husband and I were raised. When my husband is out of town, my neighbor Mr. Slaughter checks up on me and my boys. In return, I plant tomatoes near the front of the house, so as he walks home, he can pick and enjoy. I also keep him well fed with homemade desserts, and lend a helping hand when he needs it.

Fortunately, my children carry the farming gene. They help plant lettuce, cucumbers, beans, squash, and tomatoes in early spring, weed as the summer goes on, and harvest when ready. My husband revived a secondhand rototiller that I use to cultivate the soil. As I walk the rows, I visualize my dad rototilling our garden back on the family farm. Nothing is more rewarding to me than planting tiny seeds, watching them emerge from the warm, rich soil, and seeing them grow into a vegetable or fruit. My children are discovering that same satisfaction.

My husband and I are rearing our children in very much the same way our parents did us. Teaching them that hard work, long days, and much effort go into every successful task. They help muck out horse stalls, mend fences, and haul hay in from the fields before it rains. Weekly trips to sell goods at the farmers market

are a beloved ritual, a social gathering of friends and family. I rise before the sun comes up, packing homemade goodies such as Blueberry-Peach Coffee Cake (page 48), Raspberry-Rhubarb Jam (page 38), and Farmhouse Sweet Pickle Relish (page 80) for sale. Each week, I offer a different selection that I hope will keep customers coming back. Our eldest son, Camden, helps. He's learning how to count money backwards, provide pleasant customer service, and about food safety and marketing. I learned many of the same things working with my parents in my early farm life. It gives me great joy to see the cycle continuing, and to share the flavor and love of my farm life through this book.

Just as the cycle of farm life continues in our family, what's old is new and trending again in the wider world—simpler ways of living, hanging laundry on a clothesline outside, limiting technology, and making meals together as a family. I hope this cookbook will inspire you to prepare farm-fresh home-cooked meals with your own family. I'm fortunate to have recipes for my mother's cakes and breads, such as Old-Fashioned Oatmeal Bread (page 121), plus those of my grandmothers' and some family friends. I'm delighted to share them with you, along with those I developed in my Carolina kitchen. Home-cooked meals like these bring families and communities together—back around the kitchen table with device-free conversation. Simple dishes using farm-fresh eggs, locally grown produce, and ingredients you have in the pantry are the ones I love best. Maybe you'll plant a few additional heirloom tomato varieties this season, make homemade marinara sauce, and can it for the first time. Or maybe you'll try your hand at making sourdough bread served with a jar of your own berry jam. Whatever you do, have fun and enjoy the time with family and friends sharing wholesome, simple dishes.

FARMING ROOTS HOMESPUN FAMILY TRADITIONS

FRENCH-CANADIAN AND POLISH FARMING ROOTS ARE STRONG IN OUR FAMILY. When I was growing up, meals featured heirloom recipes—especially baked goods—that had been passed down many generations on handwritten recipe cards. Some of the recipes were written in French and had been translated. But the message of their flavors was universal: The joy of family and friends gathered around the kitchen table for a home-cooked meal. Deep rural history was etched into those handwritten recipes. Much of my own recipe development is inspired by the many handwritten recipes that have been passed down by multiple generations.

Farm families will drop anything to help one another. If we weren't working on our own farm, we would often be at another lending a helping hand. A neighboring farm might need a few extra sets of hands to put up hay before it rains, and another may have a leaky roof that everyone pitches in to help repair. After a hard day's work, food brings us all together. One year, a family living near mine had not stocked firewood for the winter because the father had been sick with pneumonia. A woodstove was the family's only source of heat in the bitter Connecticut winter. Other farm families united to split and stack firewood while the father recovered. A cast iron pot of homemade beef stew, root vegetables, and homemade cornbread kept our bellies full as we worked to see that these folks had what they needed. We knew they would do the same for us if need be. We often shared meals that were farm grown. The antibiotic-free pork was raised on our own farm along with many vegetables. Homemade marinara sauce was made and put up in dozens of Ball Mason jars to get us through the cold winter months. The self-sufficiency skills we learned as children motivated and molded us to become entrepreneurs as adults.

When spring planting time arrived, my brother and I helped plant heirloom tomato plants, sweet peppers, pickling cucumbers, eggplant, and other vegetables. My

father used his tool and die tradesman skills to make sprinklers for the garden out of five-gallon buckets filled with concrete, pipe, and sprinkler heads. A neighbor let us collect water from his brook, which we hauled back to the farm in a five-hundred-gallon sap tank, enabling us to water the garden. The garden's soil was enriched with compost that included manure from our own hogs. Handcrafted wire tomato cages kept tomatoes up off the ground to help eliminate disease, bugs, and bottom-end rot. Scrap rebar supported the tomato stakes, which we pounded into the ground with a post driver Dad welded in the workshop on our farm. The wire cages were secured to the rebar poles with bailing twine. When we harvested tomatoes, we used five-gallon food-safe plastic buckets and processed them at our picnic table.

I encourage you to get a small sense of farm life by growing your own vegetable garden. Choose an area that gets plenty of full sun. Add compost and till the soil. For more urban areas, community garden plots are a great idea, or grow vegetables and herbs in containers or raised beds.

FARMHOUSE MONTE CRISTO

MAKES 2 SANDWICHES

This sandwich was inspired by one at our favorite deli—Camden Deli in Camden, Maine. Try using my Farmhouse Sourdough Bread (page 122) for an amazing sandwich.

2 large eggs
1 tablespoon whole milk
Freshly ground black pepper, to taste
2 tablespoons stone-ground mustard
2 tablespoons mayonnaise
4 slices sourdough bread
6 thin slices honey ham
½ cup grated sharp cheddar cheese
½ cup grated Gruyère cheese
2 tablespoons butter

Using a fork, beat the eggs with the milk and sprinkle with pepper.

Spread 1 tablespoon of mustard evenly on 1 slice of bread. Spread 1 tablespoon of mayonnaise evenly on a second slice of bread. Repeat with the remaining 2 slices of bread. Place 3 slices of ham, ¼ cup of Gruyère, and ¼ cup of cheddar onto each mustard slice. Top with the mayonnaise slice and press down slightly on the sandwiches.

Heat a skillet over medium heat and melt the butter. Dip and coat both sides of the sandwiches in the egg mixture and place them in the skillet. Cook for 2–3 minutes on each side, until golden brown and the cheese is melted.

RUSTIC APPLE FRENCH TOAST BAKE

» SERVES 8 TO 10

This make-ahead casserole will be a favorite in your household. A medley of tart apples and warm cinnamon topped with the flavor of sweet maple syrup will make a special breakfast.

FRENCH TOAST

1 day-old baguette

2 ½ cups whole milk

1 cup heavy whipping cream

9 large eggs

¼ cup pure maple syrup

2 teaspoons pure vanilla extract

1 teaspoon ground cinnamon

½ teaspoon ground nutmeg

1 teaspoon kosher salt

APPLE TOPPING

5 to 6 large baking apples (such as Macoun or Granny Smith), peeled, cored, and thinly sliced

2 tablespoons freshly squeezed lemon juice

¼ cup pure maple syrup, plus more for drizzling

½ teaspoon ground cinnamon

3 tablespoons unsalted butter, melted

STREUSEL TOPPING

¼ cup (½ stick) unsalted butter

½ cup granulated maple sugar

1 cup all-purpose flour

1 teaspoon ground cinnamon

½ teaspoon ground nutmeg

Powdered sugar, for dusting

Prepare a 9 x 13-inch ceramic baking dish by spraying with cooking spray or brushing with softened butter.

FRENCH TOAST Cut the baguette into 1-inch-thick slices and transfer them to the baking dish. In a medium bowl, whisk together the milk, cream, and eggs. Whisk in the maple syrup, vanilla, cinnamon, nutmeg, and salt. Pour the egg mixture over the bread.

APPLE TOPPING Place the apple slices in a medium bowl and toss with the lemon juice, maple syrup, cinnamon, and butter. Spread the apple mixture evenly over the bread. Cover the baking dish with plastic wrap and refrigerate overnight.

STREUSEL TOPPING Place all the ingredients in a bowl and combine well with your hands. Cover with plastic wrap or transfer to a ziplock bag and set aside.

When ready to cook, sprinkle on the streusel topping, and then place the baking dish in the oven and set the temperature to 375 degrees F. (Do not preheat the oven, or you may crack the dish.) Bake for 65–70 minutes, until the apples are soft and the eggs are set. The casserole is done when a butter knife inserted into the center comes out clean.

Remove from the oven, scoop into serving bowls, dust with powdered sugar, and drizzle with additional maple syrup.

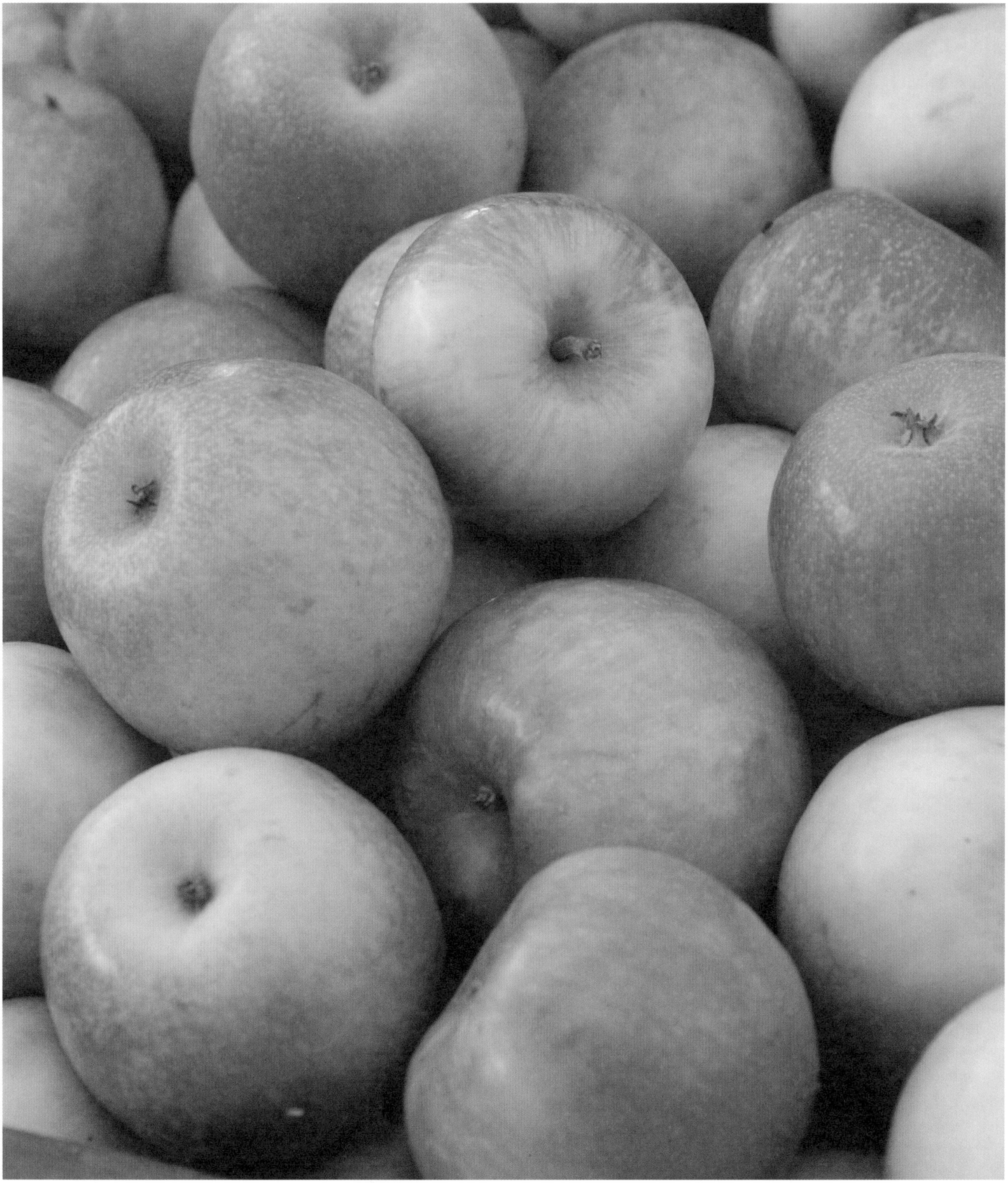

FARMER'S QUICHE

»» SERVES 8

On our farm, it always seemed there wasn't enough time in the day. My mom would often make homemade quiche, because it was quick and used ingredients we had on hand. The quiche was beautiful in one of the vintage pie dishes she had collected over the years.

CRUST

1 1/2 cups all-purpose flour

1 1/2 cups yellow cornmeal

1 teaspoon kosher salt

2 teaspoons granulated sugar

2/3 cup lard

4 tablespoons unsalted butter, cold

5 to 6 tablespoons ice water

FILLING

2 tablespoons butter

1 medium onion, sliced

2 teaspoons honey

Salt and freshly ground black pepper, to taste

1 1/2 cups fresh spinach

4 slices cooked bacon, chopped

3 to 4 slices honey ham, chopped

1 cup grated cheddar or pizza blend cheese

1 cup whole milk

1 cup heavy whipping cream

5 large eggs

1 teaspoon garlic powder

2 to 3 heirloom tomatoes, sliced

CRUST Combine the flour, cornmeal, salt, and sugar in a medium bowl. Stir to combine. Cut in the lard and butter using a pastry cutter or two forks. Add the water, 1 tablespoon at a time, until the crust holds together when squeezed in your hand. Transfer the crust to a large ziplock bag and refrigerate for 1–2 hours.

FILLING Melt the butter in a sauté pan over low to medium heat. Add the onion to the pan, stirring occasionally with a wooden spoon. Cook over low to medium heat for about 15 minutes. Add the honey and sprinkle with salt and pepper. Turn off heat and set aside.

Preheat oven to 425 degrees F.

To finish the crust, press the cornmeal mixture into a 10-inch cast iron skillet with your hands. Gently poke holes in the bottom with a fork. Bake for 12 minutes. Let cool for 10 minutes. Reduce the oven temperature to 375 degrees F.

To finish the filling, place the spinach, bacon, ham, cheese, and caramelized onion into the crust. Set aside. In a large measuring cup, combine the milk and cream. Add the eggs, salt and pepper, and garlic powder and beat well with a fork. Pour the mixture into the crust. Gently place the tomato slices in a circular pattern on the top of the quiche.

Bake for about 60 minutes, until the eggs are set and the top is golden brown. Let cool for 15–20 minutes before slicing.

OLD-FASHIONED DOUGHNUTS

» MAKES 18 DOUGHNUTS AND HOLES

This simple, old-fashioned doughnut recipe comes from our farm kitchen. My mom made these yummy treats all the time when I was growing up. You can make the doughnuts the night before, place them on baking sheets, cover with plastic wrap, and refrigerate. In the morning, you can fry them up fresh.

6 tablespoons unsalted butter, softened

½ cup granulated sugar

½ cup firmly packed brown sugar

2 large eggs, room temperature

1 teaspoon pure vanilla extract

4 ¾ to 5 cups all-purpose or cake flour

1 tablespoon baking powder

1 teaspoon baking soda

¼ teaspoon ground nutmeg

⅛ teaspoon ground allspice

1 teaspoon kosher salt

1 cup buttermilk

Canola oil, for frying

Powdered sugar, for dusting (optional)

Cinnamon sugar, for rolling (optional)

Line 2 baking sheets with parchment paper and set aside.

In a large mixing bowl, use a mixer to cream together the butter, granulated sugar, and brown sugar. Add the eggs one at a time, mixing after each addition, and then add the vanilla.

Sift the flour, baking powder, baking soda, nutmeg, allspice, and salt into a medium bowl.

Alternate adding the buttermilk and dry ingredients to the butter mixture until everything is combined, occasionally scraping the sides of the bowl with a rubber spatula.

Turn the dough out onto a lightly floured work surface. Lightly flour the top of the dough as you work, so your rolling pin does not stick. Roll out to about ½ inch thick and use a doughnut cutter to cut out the doughnuts. Place the doughnuts and doughnut holes on the prepared baking sheets.

Line another baking sheet with several layers of paper towels and set aside.

In a large pot, heat about 3 inches of oil to 375 degrees F. Drop about 4 doughnuts into the hot oil at a time, but do not overcrowd the pot. Cook for 1–2 minutes on each side, flipping the doughnuts once. Remove doughnuts from the oil and let drain on the paper towels.

Dust the doughnuts with powdered sugar after fully cooled, or roll in cinnamon sugar while still warm.

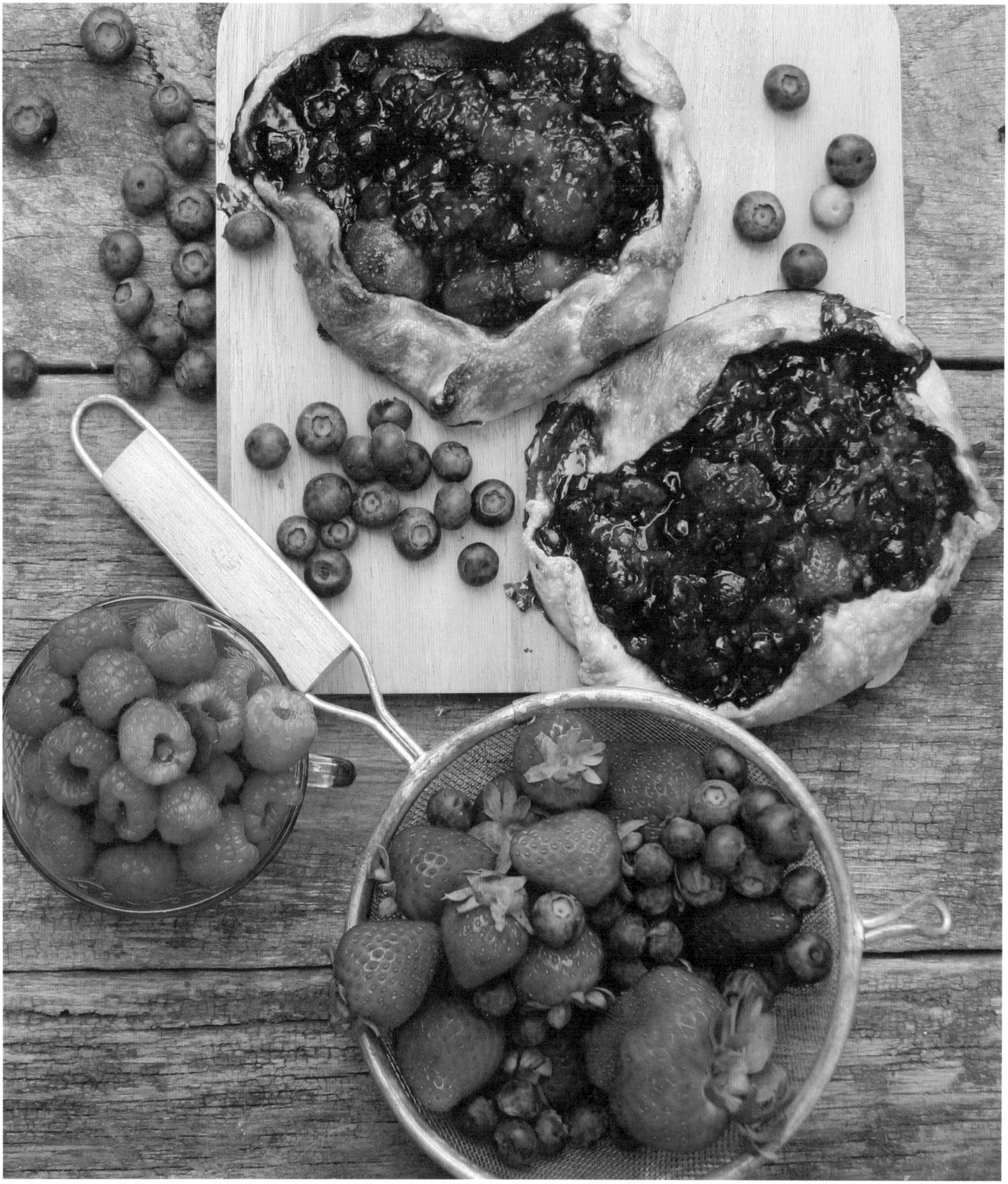

MIXED BERRY GALETTES

SERVES 6 TO 8

These rustic free-formed pies are perfect for a simple dessert. To make them special, top with vanilla ice cream and freshly whipped cream. For a very flaky crust, be sure to keep the dough very cold and do not overwork. These also bake well in 6-inch cast iron skillets as individual desserts.

- 2 cups all-purpose flour
- 1 teaspoon kosher salt
- 1 tablespoon granulated sugar
- ½ cup (1 stick) unsalted butter, cold
- 4 ounces cream cheese, cold
- ¼ cup ice water
- 1 cup fresh blueberries
- 1 cup fresh raspberries
- 1 cup sliced fresh strawberries
- 2 tablespoons freshly squeezed lemon juice
- ¾ cup granulated sugar
- 3 tablespoons instant tapioca
- 1 large egg mixed with 1 teaspoon cold water
- Vanilla ice cream, for serving
- Whipped cream, for serving

In a large bowl, combine the flour, salt, and sugar. Using a pastry cutter or two forks, cut in the butter and cream cheese until you have pea-size pieces. Add a little cold water at a time until you can gently squeeze the mixture together with your hands. Place the dough in a large ziplock bag and refrigerate for 2–3 hours or overnight.

In a large bowl, combine the berries, lemon juice, sugar, and tapioca. Stir gently with a spoon and set aside.

Line a half sheet pan with parchment paper. On a lightly floured work surface, roll out the dough into 6–8 ¼-inch-thick rounds. Transfer the rounds to the sheet pan.

Preheat the oven to 400 degrees F.

Spoon the fruit mixture evenly onto the center of each pastry. Fold up edges, crimping gently as you go. The berry filling should still be visible. Brush the edges with the egg wash. Bake for 25–30 minutes, until crust is golden brown and fruit is bubbly. Let cool slightly. Serve topped with vanilla ice cream and whipped cream.

MAPLE PEANUT BRITTLE

»» SERVES 12

One of our most popular maple confections at the sugarhouse is this old-fashioned candy. The splash of maple syrup in this particular recipe gives it a unique flavor. It's best to make this candy in a cool, dry environment so that it sets properly.

- Vegetable oil, for greasing saucepan
- 1 cup granulated sugar
- 1 cup light corn syrup
- 1 cup pure maple syrup
- 1 teaspoon kosher salt
- 1 ½ cups water
- 2 teaspoons pure vanilla extract
- 1 ½ cups salted peanuts
- 2 teaspoons baking soda

Grease 2 half sheet pans and a rubber spatula. Set aside.

Using a paper towel, brush the top inside edge of a medium saucepan with oil. Over medium heat, dissolve the sugar, corn syrup, maple syrup, salt, and water in the saucepan. Stir continuously with a wooden spoon until mixture comes to a boil. Reduce heat to medium low and continue cooking, without stirring, until the candy thermometer reaches 290–295 degrees F. It's important to closely watch this mixture while it cooks. Once it starts climbing in temperature, it can burn quickly.

When the mixture reaches temperature, remove the pan from the heat. Quickly stir in the vanilla, peanuts, and baking soda. Pour immediately onto prepared baking pans. Spread the mixture on the sheet pan with the prepared spatula. Carefully, use the spatula and your hands to pull the candy, stretching it thin. You will need to work quickly. Once the candy is cooled, crack it into pieces using your hands. Transfer to a ziplock bag or plastic container. Store in a cool, dry place for up to 4–6 months.

FARMHOUSE MARBLE CAKE

MAKES 2 LOAF CAKES

This cake is inspired by the one my mom used to bake. Simple and old-fashioned pound cakes with swirls of vanilla and chocolate were a tradition in our household.

- 1 ½ cups (3 sticks) unsalted butter, softened
- 2 cups granulated sugar
- 2 teaspoons pure vanilla extract
- 5 large eggs, room temperature
- 1 cup full-fat sour cream
- 3 cups all-purpose or cake flour
- 1 teaspoon kosher salt
- ½ teaspoon baking powder
- 2 ounces unsweetened baking chocolate

Preheat the oven to 350 degrees F. Spray two 9 x 5-inch loaf pans with cooking spray and set aside. For easier removal of the cakes, use paper liners.

In the bowl of a stand mixer, or in a large bowl using an electric hand mixer, cream together the butter, sugar, and vanilla. Add the eggs one at a time, mixing after each addition. Add the sour cream and combine, occasionally scraping the sides of the bowl with a rubber spatula. Sift together the flour, salt, and baking powder. Add the flour mixture to the butter mixture and combine, scraping the sides of the bowl as needed. Transfer a third of the batter to a separate bowl.

Melt the chocolate in either a small saucepan over low heat on the stovetop, or in the microwave at 30-second intervals. Allow to cool slightly. Stir the chocolate into the reserved third of batter. Scoop the batter evenly into the prepared pans, alternating between the chocolate and vanilla. Using a butter knife, swirl the cake batters together to create a marble pattern. Do not touch the sides or bottoms of the pans when swirling.

Bake for 55–60 minutes, until a toothpick inserted into the center comes out clean. Transfer cakes to a cooling rack and cool completely before removing from the pans.

RED VELVET MARBLE CAKE

» 12 SERVINGS

This cake was inspired by Southerners' love for red velvet cake, and my love of Nordic Ware's Bundt pans. Twisted and swirled with old-fashioned cake batter, this one is a keeper.

- 1 cup (2 sticks) unsalted butter, softened
- 2 ½ cups granulated sugar
- 2 teaspoons pure vanilla extract
- 6 large eggs, room temperature
- 1 ½ cups full-fat sour cream
- 3 cups all-purpose or cake flour
- 1 teaspoon kosher salt
- 2 teaspoons baking powder
- ⅓ cup unsweetened cocoa powder
- 1 teaspoon apple cider vinegar
- 1 teaspoon red food coloring
- ½ teaspoon baking soda

Preheat the oven to 350 degrees F. Spray a 12-cup Bundt pan with nonstick baking spray, or brush with shortening, and dust with flour. Carefully tap out any excess flour.

In the bowl of a stand mixer, or in a large bowl using an electric hand mixer, cream together the butter, sugar, and vanilla. Add the eggs one at a time, mixing after each addition. Add the sour cream and combine, occasionally scraping the sides of the bowl with a rubber spatula.

In a medium bowl, sift the flour, salt, and baking powder together. Add the flour mixture to the butter mixture and mix well. Transfer a third of the batter to a separate bowl. Gently fold in the cocoa powder, vinegar, food coloring, and baking soda into the reserved third of batter.

Scoop the batter into the prepared Bundt pan, alternating between red velvet and vanilla. Using a butter knife, swirl the cake batters together to create a marble pattern. Do not touch the sides or bottoms of the pan when swirling.

Bake for 55–60 minutes, until a toothpick inserted into the center comes out clean. Cool the cake in the pan on a cooling rack for 10 minutes. Remove from the pan and let cool completely.

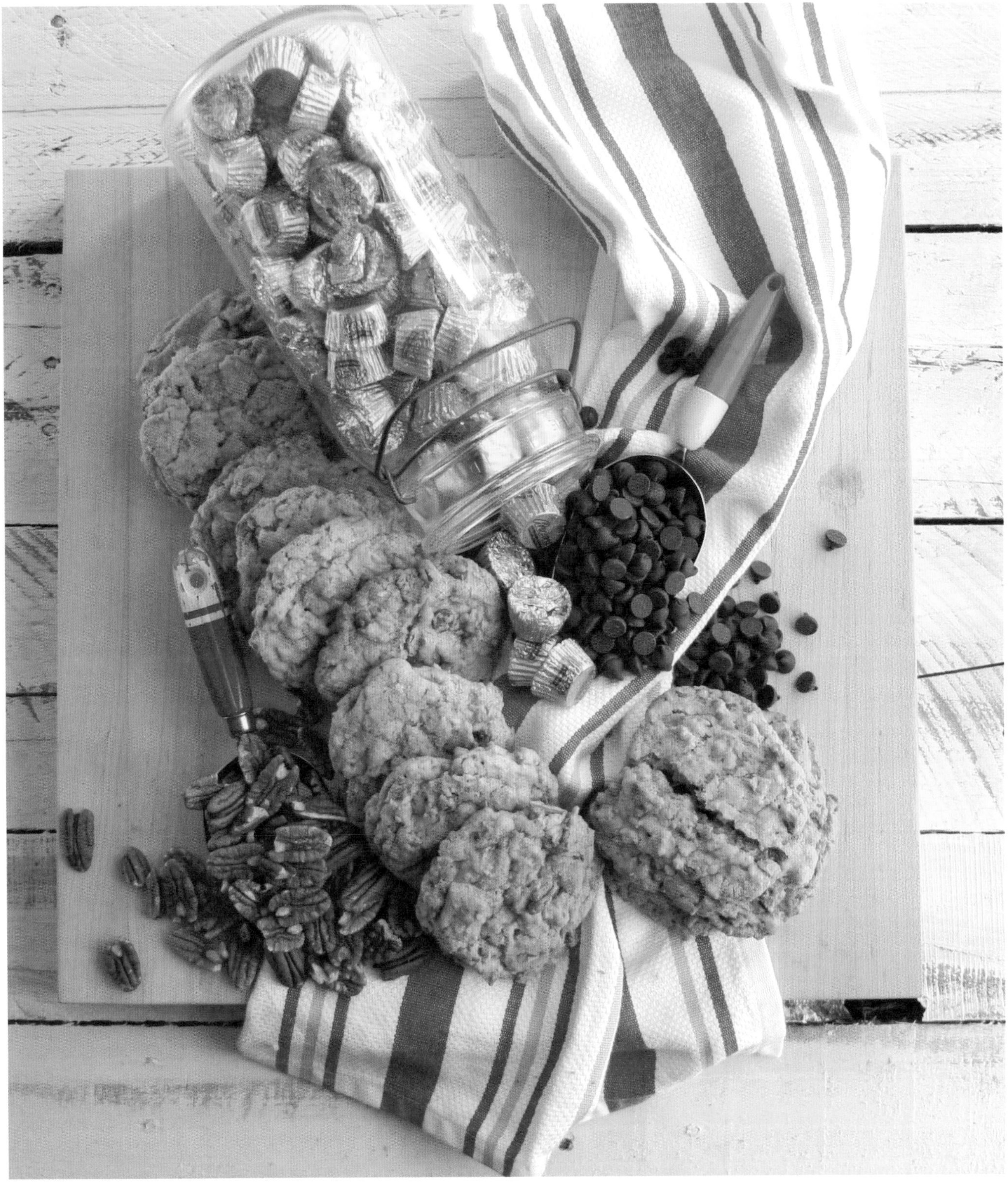

FARMGIRL PANTRY COOKIES

MAKES ABOUT 36 COOKIES

This delicious cookie came about when I was trying to use up some leftover Easter candies. Who doesn't love a chewy and gooey chocolate chip cookie? Add chopped pecans and pieces of peanut butter cups and we're completely in love.

- 1 cup (2 sticks) unsalted butter, softened
- 1 cup granulated sugar
- 1 cup firmly packed brown sugar
- 1 teaspoon pure vanilla extract
- 2 large eggs, room temperature
- 2 ½ cups all-purpose flour
- 1 ½ cups old-fashioned rolled oats
- 1 teaspoon kosher salt
- 1 teaspoon baking soda
- 1 teaspoon baking powder
- ¾ cup chopped pecans
- ¾ cup semisweet chocolate chips
- 12 to 14 Reese's Peanut Butter Cups Miniatures, cut into small pieces

Preheat the oven to 375 degrees F. Line 3 half sheet pans with parchment paper and set aside.

In the bowl of a stand mixer, or in a large bowl using an electric mixer, cream together the butter, granulated sugar, and brown sugar. Add the vanilla and eggs and combine. Add the flour, oats, salt, baking soda, and baking powder; incorporate well, occasionally scraping the bottom and sides of the mixing bowl with a rubber spatula. Toss in the pecans, chocolate chips, and peanut butter cup pieces and incorporate.

Scoop cookie dough by the tablespoonful onto the prepared sheet pans with about 4 rows of 3 cookies each. Bake for 14–15 minutes, until lightly golden brown. Let cool slightly on the pans before transferring to cooling racks to cool completely.

WHAT'S IN SEASON THE FARMERS MARKET LIFE

EACH SUNDAY FROM MAY UNTIL THE END OF OCTOBER, I WOULD HELP MY DAD SELL MAPLE SYRUP, BERRY JAMS, AND OTHER HOMEMADE CONFECTIONS AT THE FARMERS MARKET. My family started out making maple syrup but soon realized that most people don't need maple syrup every week, so we developed other products. As the family business progressed, we created unique maple-inspired confections, jams, and sauces to diversify our product line. My dad made a multilevel wooden riser from reclaimed boards off the exterior of the sugarhouse, which beautifully displayed clear glass jars of jam, spice rubs, and thick savory-sweet barbeque sauce. My floral design skills helped me to create eye-catching displays for all of our farm-made products. The wooden riser was open in the back, allowing us to neatly stow away shopping bags, the money box, and other essentials.

When I moved to North Carolina a few years back, I wanted to start selling jams, jellies, and baked goods. Using the skills and knowledge I had obtained from many years of assisting my parents at county fairs and farmers markets, I set out to start my own venture. After obtaining the required licenses, I got to work. Now, from April through late November, I set up a stand at the local farmers market. Each week, what I offer changes in the hope of keeping customers coming back. I am a very observant person and watch the way customers shop the market. I keep a handwritten journal, taking notes on the products I made, what sold, weather conditions, how customers responded to a new product, and my income. People get bored quickly, so I mix it up every week, attempting to pique their interest. I've also noticed that people tend to love items they can consume immediately, and my Southern-Fried Apple Hand Pies (page 164) sell out fast.

I bake one type of cookie each week, rotating between four or five different varieties. I also offer something for customers to drink, complimentary. What I offer depends

on the season and the weather. During the early spring I offer hot coffee. In summer, I mix it up with citrus-mint infused water, peach sweet tea, and strawberry or blueberry lemonade. In the fall, a cup of hot mulled apple cider hits the spot.

My husband built me a wooden step, similar to the one my dad uses at the farmers markets in Connecticut, that displays jars of jam, barbeque sauce, and pickles. Baked goods lay on the table in front of that. Vintage-style chalkboards let customers know what I have and what it costs. I love using canvas drop cloths for my table linens because they are neutral in color, durable, and washable. Then I add depth of interest with burlap grain bags and various dishcloths. If you put attention and detail into your display, people take notice.

The farmers market is more than a great place to buy locally produced food directly from the hands of those who grow it. It's a social gathering of friends and family. As a vendor, I arrive about an hour early with my oldest son, Camden, to set up. He's learning customer service skills, food safety, reliability, and responsibility. Camden loves helping set up and waiting on customers. By working at the market, he is also earning horseback riding lessons. I pay him each week, and he must save the money to pay for lessons himself.

As the market draws to a close, many farmers are ready to deal. I often trade baked goods for free-range eggs, heirloom tomatoes, other vegetables, and antibiotic-free pork. You might be able to get a bulk discount on berries for jam—just ask. Often, if there's impending bad weather, farmers have no other option but to harvest everything ripe that week and are looking to offload produce quickly. Berries and stone fruit freeze exceptionally well. We have an upright freezer in our garage to store berries at their peak of ripeness for when I'm ready to turn them into jams, jellies, pies, and other baked goods. Many of the recipes featured in this chapter are ones that I created to sell at the market. Others utilize fresh berries and produce available from farmers at your local market.

BLUEBERRY OATMEAL PANCAKES

SERVES 4 TO 5

We love making breakfast at home, and these yummy pancakes are no exception. Top with warm maple syrup and freshly whipped cream, dust with ground cinnamon, and your breakfast will be complete. If you can find them, we adore wild blueberries in this recipe.

4 large eggs
1 1/2 cups whole milk
2 cups buttermilk
1 teaspoon pure vanilla extract
1/3 cup melted butter or vegetable oil
2 1/2 cups all-purpose flour
3 tablespoons granulated sugar
1 1/2 teaspoons baking soda
2 teaspoons baking powder
1 teaspoon kosher salt
3/4 cup old-fashioned rolled oats
1 cup fresh blueberries
Butter, for serving
Maple syrup, warm, for serving

Heat a griddle pan or large skillet over medium heat. Grease with butter or cooking spray.

In the bowl of a stand mixer, or in a large bowl using an electric hand mixer, beat the eggs, milk, buttermilk, and vanilla until foamy, 2–3 minutes on high speed. Stir in the melted butter.

Sift together the flour, sugar, baking soda, baking powder, and salt into a medium bowl. Add the oats and pour in the egg mixture. Gently fold together with a rubber spatula. The batter will be slightly lumpy.

Preheat the oven to 200 degrees F. Line a half sheet pan with parchment paper and place in the oven.

Using a ladle, scoop about 1/2 cup of the batter onto the hot griddle pan. Sprinkle a small handful of blueberries into each pancake. Cook the pancakes until they bubble around the edges, about 2 minutes. Flip over and cook the other side until golden brown, about another 2 minutes. As each pancake is finished, place it on the sheet pan in the oven to keep warm.

Serve with butter and warm maple syrup.

BERRY-SWIRLED POPS

» MAKES 10 POPS

Creamy yogurt and fresh berries are swirled together to make hot summer days a bit cooler with these refreshing pops. They are also very pretty. I found the best ice pop mold on Amazon.

½ cup fresh or frozen blueberries

½ cup fresh or frozen raspberries

½ cup fresh or frozen whole strawberries

2 cups full-fat Greek yogurt (plain or vanilla)

¼ cup honey

2 tablespoons freshly squeezed lemon juice

In a medium saucepan over medium heat, cook the berries until they are soft, 15–20 minutes. Remove from heat, put softened berry mixture into a blender, and purée. Let cool to room temperature.

In a large measuring bowl, stir together the yogurt, honey, and lemon juice. Swirl the cooled fruit mixture into the yogurt mixture, creating a marble effect.

Pour the yogurt-berry mixture into 10 ice pop molds. Cover molds with lids and insert wooden craft sticks. Freeze until firm, 3–4 hours or overnight. When they are fully frozen, run the bottom of the molds under warm water to easily remove the ice pops. Serve immediately, or store the pops in freezer-proof bags for up to 1–2 months.

STRAWBERRY-BLUEBERRY POPS

» MAKES 10 POPS

Pops are one of the easiest treats to make with your kids. If you prepare a bunch ahead of time, you will be ready for any hot summer afternoon or picnic.

- 1 cup fresh or frozen blueberries
- 1 cup fresh or frozen sliced strawberries
- 1 cup water
- 2 tablespoons granulated sugar
- 1 (3-ounce) package strawberry or raspberry Jell-O
- ¼ cup freshly squeezed lemon juice

In a medium saucepan over medium heat, cook the blueberries, strawberries, and water until the fruit is softened. Press the fruit and water mixture through a sieve. Discard the pulp and seeds and reserve the juice.

Return the berry juice to the saucepan and bring to a simmer over medium heat. When the juice reaches a simmer, remove the pan from the heat. Add the sugar, Jell-O, and lemon juice; whisk until the sugar and Jell-O are dissolved.

Transfer the liquid to a large measuring cup and pour into ice pop molds. Cover molds with lids and insert wooden craft sticks. Freeze until firm, 3–4 hours or overnight. When they are fully frozen, run the bottom of the mold under warm water to easily remove the ice pops. Serve immediately, or store the pops in freezer-proof bags for up to 1–2 months.

RASPBERRY-RHUBARB JAM

MAKES 10 (8-OUNCE) JARS

With a great love of raspberries in our family, we developed this yummy jam. Sweet and tart, it reminds me of harvesting rhubarb in the misting rain on the edge of our vegetable garden on my parents' farm.

- 5 ½ cups fresh or frozen raspberries
- 2 cups chopped rhubarb (1-inch pieces)
- 7 cups granulated sugar, divided
- 1 (1.75-ounce) package fruit pectin*
- 2 tablespoons freshly squeezed lemon juice

*Pomona's Universal Pectin is my preferred choice for pectin. It's available in stores or online.

**Granulated vegetable defoamer can be purchased from most maple syrup equipment suppliers. This product helps eliminate foam from your jams, jellies, and preserves but does not add dairy contamination as using butter will.

In a 6- to 8-quart saucepan over low to medium heat, cook the raspberries and rhubarb until soft. Lightly smash the fruit with a potato masher and set the pan aside.

Prepare a boiling water canner. Heat the jars and lids in simmering water until ready for use. Do not boil. Set bands aside.

In a glass measuring cup, combine 2 cups of the sugar with the pectin. Add the lemon juice and sugar-pectin mixture to the berries. Over high heat, bring the mixture to a full rolling boil that cannot be stirred down, stirring frequently with a wooden spoon. Boil for 1 minute. Immediately add the remaining 5 cups sugar and bring back to a full boil for 1 minute, stirring constantly. Turn the heat to low to keep the jam warm. Skim foam if necessary. (You can also use granulated vegetable defoamer,** if needed, to help eliminate any foam.)

Ladle hot jam into hot jars, leaving ½-inch headspace. Wipe the rims with a clean, damp paper towel. Center the lids on the jars. Apply the bands until the fit is fingertip tight. Process jars in the boiling water canner for 10 minutes, adjusting for altitude. Remove the jars and allow to cool. (I use a pair of rubber-tipped tongs to easily handle hot jars.) Check the lids for seal after 24 hours. The lid should not flex up and down when the center is pressed. Store jars in a cool, dry place. If a jar doesn't seal, store in the refrigerator for up to 8 weeks.

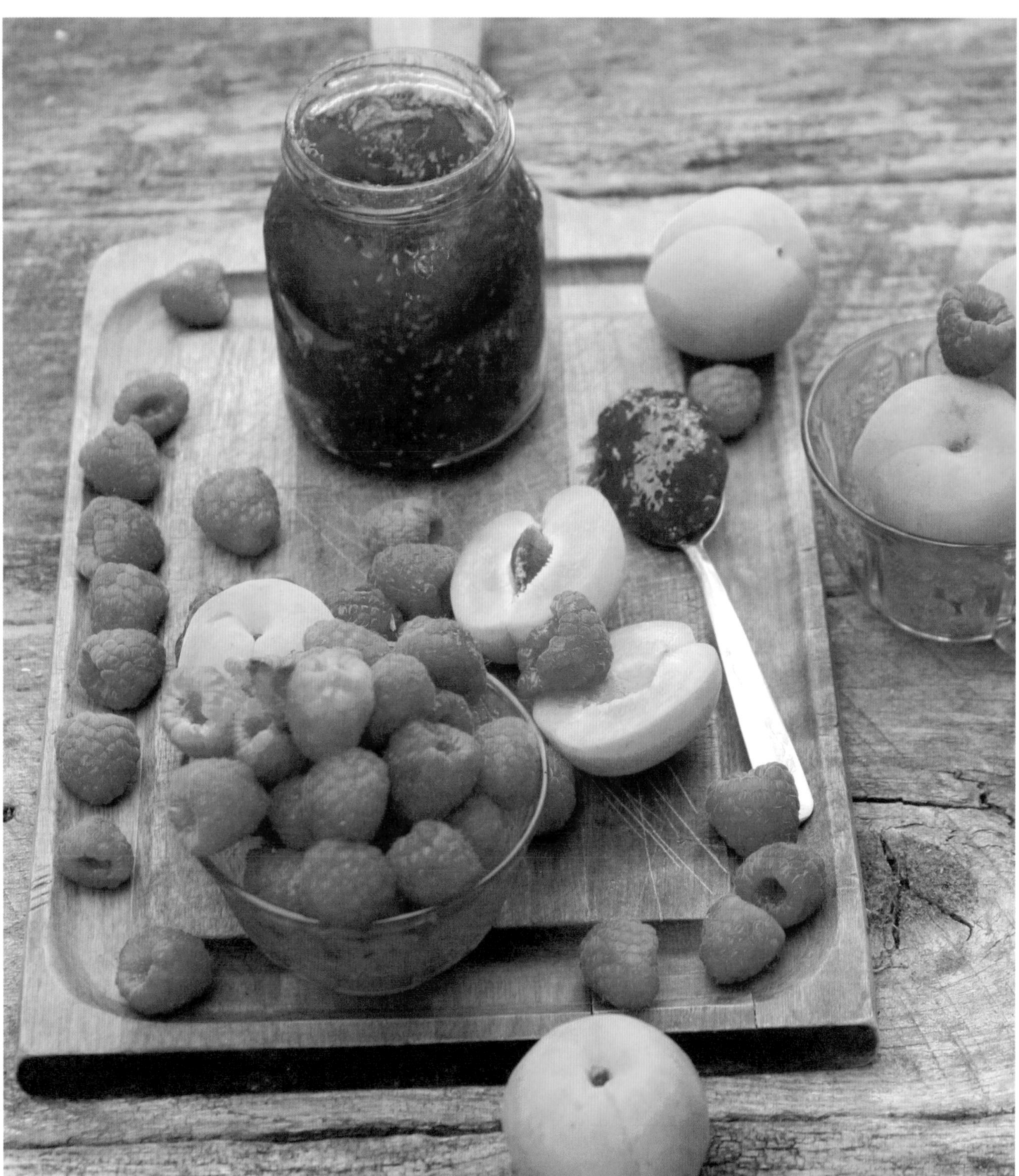

RASPBERRY-APRICOT JAM

» MAKES 12 (8-OUNCE) JARS

Here, two of my dad's favorite fruits are blended together to make an amazing jam. Black raspberry bushes grew on the sides of the driveway on my parents' farm. We would pick those berries and make homemade jam and fruit roll-ups.

- 4 cups fresh raspberries
- 3 ½ cups pitted and quartered apricots
- 6 cups granulated sugar, divided
- 1 (1.75-ounce) package fruit pectin*
- 3 tablespoons freshly squeezed lemon juice

*Pomona's Universal Pectin is my preferred choice for pectin. It's available in stores or online.

**Granulated vegetable defoamer can be purchased from most maple syrup equipment suppliers. This product helps eliminate foam from your jams, jellies, and preserves but does not add dairy contamination as using butter will.

In a 6- to 8-quart saucepan over low to medium heat, cook the raspberries and apricot pieces until soft. Lightly smash the fruit with a potato masher and set the pan aside.

Prepare a boiling water canner. Heat the jars and lids in simmering water until ready for use. Do not boil. Set bands aside.

In a glass measuring cup, combine 2 cups of the sugar with the pectin. Add the lemon juice and sugar-pectin mixture to the berries. Over high heat, bring the mixture to a full rolling boil that cannot be stirred down, stirring frequently with a wooden spoon. Boil for 1 minute. Immediately add the remaining 4 cups sugar and bring back to a full boil for 1 minute, stirring constantly. Turn the heat to low to keep the jam warm. Skim foam if necessary. (You can also use a granulated vegetable defoamer,** if needed, to help eliminate any foam.)

Ladle hot jam into hot jars, leaving ½-inch headspace. Wipe the rims with a clean, damp paper towel. Center the lids on the jars. Apply the bands until the fit is fingertip tight. Process jars in the boiling water canner for 10 minutes, adjusting for altitude. Remove the jars and allow to cool. (I use a pair of rubber-tipped tongs to easily handle hot jars.) Check the lids for seal after 24 hours. The lid should not flex up and down when the center is pressed. Store jars in a cool, dry place. If a jar doesn't seal, store in the refrigerator for up to 8 weeks.

CRANBERRY, APRICOT, AND NUT GRANOLA BARS

» MAKES 15 TO 18 BARS

These homemade chewy granola bars are great nutritious snacks for day trips. You can get creative and add raisins, shredded coconut, chocolate chips, and other dried fruit.

4 cups old-fashioned rolled oats
1 ½ cups all-purpose flour
1 teaspoon kosher salt
1 teaspoon baking powder
½ cup firmly packed brown sugar
½ cup chopped dried apricots
½ cup dried cranberries
½ cup sunflower seeds
½ cup chopped pecans
½ cup chopped walnuts
1 teaspoon pure vanilla extract
½ cup pure maple syrup or honey
½ cup (1 stick) butter, softened, or vegetable oil
1 large egg

Line a 9 x 13-inch pan with parchment paper and lightly spray with cooking spray. Preheat the oven to 350 degrees F.

In a large bowl, combine the oats, flour, salt, baking powder, brown sugar, apricots, cranberries, sunflower seeds, pecans, and walnuts. Add the vanilla, maple syrup, butter, and egg. Stir until the mixture is evenly crumbly. Spread in the prepared pan and gently pat down the mixture until flat.

Bake the bars for 25–30 minutes, until lightly golden brown. Remove from the oven and let cool in the pan for about 5 minutes on a cooling rack. Use a sharp knife or bench knife to cut the bars. Cool completely before storing in an airtight container or wrapping individually with plastic wrap. During humid weather, store bars in the refrigerator. The bars can be stored for up to 1 week.

LEMON-BLUEBERRY POUND CAKE

»» MAKES 12 SERVINGS

This is a recipe I developed to sell at the farmers market. I usually sell out of this cake every week. It is full of fresh lemon flavor thanks to pure lemon oil. Lemon oil is the very potent extract from lemon rinds with nothing added. Lemon extract, on the other hand, contains water and alcohol.

CAKE

1 cup (2 sticks) unsalted butter, softened

2 ½ cups granulated sugar

6 large eggs, at room temperature

1 cup full-fat sour cream

¼ cup freshly squeezed lemon juice

1 tablespoon pure lemon oil

4 cups all-purpose or cake flour

1 teaspoon kosher salt

1 teaspoon baking powder

½ teaspoon baking soda

1 cup fresh or frozen (thawed and drained) blueberries

ICING

2 cups powdered sugar

1 to 2 tablespoons whole milk

2 tablespoons freshly squeezed lemon juice

Preheat the oven to 350 degrees F. Spray a 12-cup Bundt pan with cooking spray, or brush with shortening, and coat with flour. Tap the pan lightly to shake out any excess flour. Set aside.

CAKE Cream the butter and sugar in the bowl of a stand mixer, or in a large bowl using an electric hand mixer. Mix in the eggs, sour cream, lemon juice, and lemon oil, occasionally scraping the bottom and sides of the bowl with a rubber spatula. Add the flour, salt, baking powder, and baking soda and mix thoroughly. Fold in the blueberries. Pour the batter into the prepared pan. Bake for 70–75 minutes, until a toothpick inserted into the center comes out clean. Let cake cool in the pan for about 10 minutes. Turn the cake out of the pan and let cool completely on a cooling rack.

ICING Simply whisk together the ingredients in a small bowl. Add enough milk to achieve the desired thickness.

After the cake has cooled, spoon the icing over the top. Let the icing set before slicing the cake.

RUSTIC BLUEBERRY MUFFINS

» MAKES 12 MUFFINS

These blueberry muffins are moist, light, and extremely flavorful. They are perfect for breakfast, brunch, or as a treat to carry along on your busy day's adventures. A decadent rolled oat–streusel topping will have you eating every morsel.

OAT-STREUSEL TOPPING

½ cup firmly packed brown sugar

½ cup all-purpose flour

¼ cup (½ stick) unsalted butter, softened

½ cup old-fashioned rolled oats

¼ teaspoon ground cinnamon

MUFFINS

⅓ cup vegetable shortening

1 cup firmly packed brown sugar

1 teaspoon pure vanilla extract

2 large eggs

1 cup full-fat sour cream

2 cups all-purpose flour

2 teaspoons baking powder

1 teaspoon kosher salt

1 cup fresh blueberries

Preheat the oven to 375 degrees F. Line a 12-cup muffin pan with paper liners and set aside.

OAT-STREUSEL TOPPING Place all the ingredients in a medium bowl and combine well with your hands. Set aside.

MUFFINS Cream together the shortening, brown sugar, and vanilla in the bowl of a stand mixer, or in a large bowl using an electric hand mixer. Add the eggs one at a time, mixing after each addition. Scrape the bottom and the sides of the bowl occasionally with a rubber spatula. Mix in the sour cream then stir in the flour, baking powder, and salt. Fold in the blueberries using a rubber spatula.

Scoop the batter evenly into the paper liners, about three-fourths full. Sprinkle the topping evenly over the muffins. Bake for 25–30 minutes, until the tops are golden brown and a toothpick inserted into the center comes out clean. Let cool slightly before carefully removing the muffins from the pan.

RASPBERRY STREUSEL MUFFINS

»» MAKES 12 MUFFINS

These moist and flavorful muffins are the perfect addition to breakfast or brunch, or they can make a wholesome snack. Make a big batch of streusel, place it in a freezer-proof bag, and plop it in the fridge or freezer so it's at your fingertips when you want to whip up a batch.

STREUSEL TOPPING

1 cup granulated sugar

½ cup (1 stick) unsalted butter, softened

1 cup old-fashioned rolled oats

½ cup all-purpose flour

½ teaspoon ground cinnamon

MUFFINS

½ cup (1 stick) unsalted butter, softened

½ cup firmly packed brown sugar

½ cup granulated sugar

2 large eggs

1 teaspoon pure vanilla extract

1 teaspoon kosher salt

1 cup full-fat sour cream

2 cups all-purpose flour

2 teaspoons baking powder

1 cup fresh raspberries

Preheat the oven to 375 degrees F. Line a muffin pan with 12 paper liners and set aside.

STREUSEL TOPPING Place all the ingredients in a medium bowl and mix with your hands until combined. Set aside.

MUFFINS Cream the butter, brown sugar, and granulated sugar in the bowl of a stand mixer, or in a large bowl using an electric hand mixer. Add the eggs one at a time, mixing after each addition. Add the vanilla, salt, and sour cream; combine just until thoroughly mixed, occasionally scraping the bottom and sides of the bowl with a rubber spatula. Add the flour and baking powder and mix until smooth. Fold in the raspberries.

Scoop the batter evenly into the paper liners, about three-fourths full. Sprinkle the topping evenly over the muffins. Bake for 30–32 minutes, until the tops are golden brown and a toothpick inserted into the center comes out clean. Let cool slightly before removing from the pan.

BLUEBERRY-PEACH COFFEE CAKE

»» MAKES 3 LOAVES

You can substitute different fruits in this moist cake depending on what you prefer or what is in season. Blueberries and peaches blend together deliciously well.

CRUMBLE TOPPING

½ cup (1 stick) unsalted butter, softened

1 cup granulated sugar

¾ cup all-purpose flour

½ teaspoon ground cinnamon

CAKE

½ cup (1 stick) unsalted butter, softened

2 cups granulated sugar

4 large eggs, room temperature

2 teaspoons pure vanilla extract

1 ¼ cups full-fat sour cream

4 cups all-purpose or cake flour

1 tablespoon baking powder

1 teaspoon kosher salt

1 cup diced fresh peaches

1 cup fresh blueberries

CRUMBLE TOPPING Place the ingredients in a medium bowl and mix with your hands until combined. Set aside.

Preheat the oven to 350 degrees F. Spray three 9 x 5-inch loaf pans with cooking spray and set aside.

CAKE Cream together the butter and granulated sugar in the bowl of a stand mixer, or in a large bowl using an electric hand mixer. Add the eggs one at a time, mixing after each addition. Add the vanilla and sour cream and combine, occasionally scraping the bottom and sides of the bowl with a rubber spatula. Add the flour, baking powder, and salt; stir until smooth. Fold in the peaches and blueberries.

Divide the cake batter evenly among the loaf pans. Sprinkle generously with the crumble topping. Bake for 55–60 minutes, until a toothpick inserted into the centers of the cakes comes out clean. Let cool slightly in pans then transfer to a cooling rack to cool completely before slicing.

BACKYARD BARBEQUE
DOWN HOME DINNER

I LOVE BACKYARD GATHERINGS AND ENTERTAINING. A simple yet delicious meal can bring so much joy to friends and family. Add beauty to the day by picking a few loose blooms out of the garden and placing them in whatever containers you have kicking around—Mason jars, milk glasses, simple glass cylinder vases, and galvanized buckets all work well. Some of my favorite blossoms are fresh lavender, mint, hosta leaves, zinnias, scabiosa, and hydrangea. Stash paper napkins in a basket or reclaimed wood tray, and weigh them down with a clean rock to keep breezes from blowing them away. Drop disposable flatware into wide-mouth Mason jars. Old wheelbarrows, cast iron tubs, an old sink, or galvanized bins chock-full of ice hold drinks nicely. I love clear glass drink dispensers for showcasing various flavored waters, punches, or sangria. Regardless of the decor, barbeques bring people together to enjoy great company and homemade food. And that's what really matters. Outdoor meals don't have to be fancy. The point is to bring the people you love around you.

Our youngest son, Mason, has ADHD and mild autism. The teachers and staff at his school are so dedicated and caring. I wanted to do something to say thank you, so I planned a beautiful lunch for the entire staff at the school. On the day of the meal, the food was packed and ready, but my truck wouldn't start. My next door neighbor was my hero. He told us when we first moved in to call if we ever needed anything, so I did. He drove me and all of the food to the school, and he repaired the truck while I was gone. The goodness of neighbors and teachers shines through and gives me faith in the world. You can prepare the whole meal, as I did for the teachers, or you can ask your friends to bring their favorite dishes.

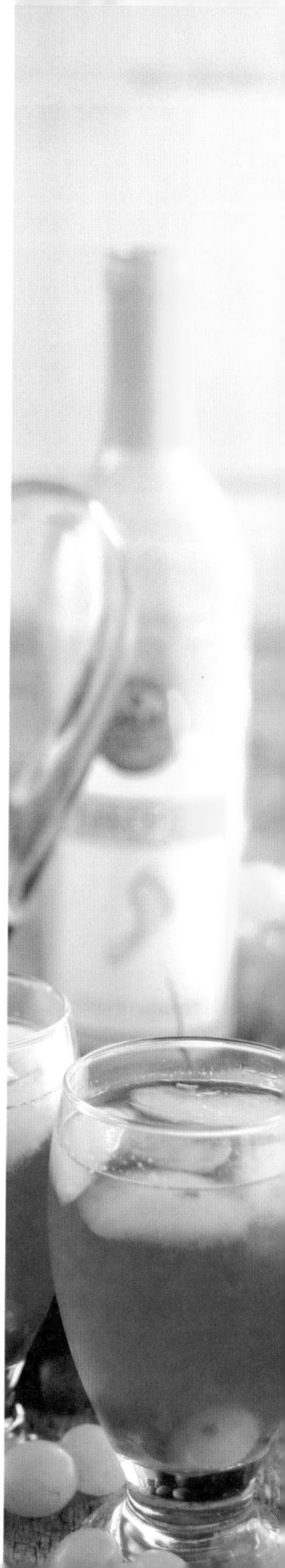

HONEY-GLAZED CARROTS

»» SERVES 4 TO 6

This is one of my absolute-favorite vegetable side dishes to go with meatloaf or a farm-cooked dinner. The simple flavors of butter, salt, and honey coat farm-fresh carrots beautifully. It's even better with carrots you harvested out of your own garden.

8 large carrots, peeled and sliced
2 tablespoons butter
2 tablespoons honey
Salt and freshly ground black pepper, to taste

Add about 1 inch of water to a medium saucepan. Add the carrots and bring to a boil. Boil for 10–12 minutes, until tender. Drain water and return the carrots to the pan.

Add the butter, honey, salt, and pepper and cook over medium heat for 6–7 minutes, until the carrots are glazed. While cooking, gently toss with a wooden spoon to coat.

MAPLE SUGAR SPICE RUB

»» MAKES ABOUT 1/2 CUP

The distinct flavors in this dry rub are wonderful on chicken, pork, or even shrimp skewers. Make it ahead of time and store in an airtight container.

3 tablespoons granulated maple sugar
2 tablespoons firmly packed brown sugar
1/4 cup freshly ground black pepper
1/4 cup kosher salt
3 tablespoons onion powder
3 tablespoons smoked paprika
1 1/2 tablespoons garlic powder
1 tablespoon chili powder
1 teaspoon ground mustard
1 teaspoon cayenne pepper
1 teaspoon ground ginger
1 teaspoon dried lemon peel

Combine all of the ingredients in a bowl and stir. Store in an airtight container in the pantry.

COUNTRY-STYLE PORK RIBS

»» SERVES 6 TO 8

I love the simplicity of this particular dish. Brown sugar caramelizes the edges of the pork and leaves you with sweet and salty flavors. Serve with Honey-Glazed Carrots (page 52) and a fresh garden salad.

- 2 tablespoons brown sugar
- 2 teaspoons onion powder
- 1 teaspoon garlic powder
- Salt and freshly ground black pepper, to taste
- 2 to 3 pounds country-style pork ribs
- 2 tablespoons extra virgin olive oil
- 1 tablespoon butter
- Prepared barbeque sauce, for serving

Preheat the oven to 400 degrees F.

Sprinkle the brown sugar, onion powder, garlic powder, salt, and pepper onto the ribs and rub into the meat. Heat an ovenproof grill pan over medium heat and add the olive oil and butter. Brown each side of the ribs, using tongs to turn the meat. Place the entire pan into the oven and roast for 20 minutes, or until the meat is cooked through. Remove from the oven and let rest for about 5 minutes before slicing. Serve the ribs with your favorite barbeque sauce for dipping.

SMOKED APPLE BARBEQUE SAUCE

»» MAKES ABOUT 4 CUPS

Homemade barbeque sauce takes no time at all to prepare and lets you control the ingredients.

- 1 cup firmly packed brown sugar
- 1 cup granulated sugar or dark maple syrup
- 1 cup apple cider vinegar
- 1 cup water
- 3/4 cup grated Honeycrisp apple
- 3/4 cup tomato paste
- 3/4 cup molasses
- 1 teaspoon liquid smoke
- 1 tablespoon onion powder
- 1 teaspoon garlic powder
- 1 tablespoon dry mustard
- 2 tablespoons freshly squeezed lemon juice
- 1/2 teaspoon cayenne pepper
- 1/2 teaspoon smoked paprika
- 1/4 teaspoon freshly ground pepper
- 1/2 teaspoon kosher salt

In a large saucepan over medium heat, whisk together all of the ingredients. Bring to a boil, stirring continuously. Allow the mixture to simmer for 20 minutes, until thickened. Transfer to a glass jar and refrigerate for up to 4 weeks, or process in a boiling water canner to make it shelf stable. The sauce will thicken as it cools.

YANKEE BARBEQUE

SERVES 8 TO 10

The first year we moved to North Carolina, I cooked lunch for all of the teachers and staff in our son Mason's elementary school. Many of them didn't know what pulled pork was. They nicknamed my dish "Yankee Barbeque." Freeze the cooked pork in 1-quart deli containers for easy meals later on.

- 1 (5- to 6-pound) boneless pork loin
- 1/4 cup stone-ground mustard
- 1/3 cup firmly packed brown sugar
- 2 teaspoons onion powder
- 1 teaspoon garlic powder
- Salt and freshly ground black pepper, to taste
- 1 cup apple cider
- Prepared barbeque sauce, for drizzling
- Kaiser rolls, for serving
- Tangy Farmhouse Coleslaw (page 55), for serving

Preheat the oven to 300 degrees F.

In a roasting pan, place the pork loin fat side up. Spread the mustard across the top of the loin. Sprinkle with brown sugar, onion powder, garlic powder, salt, and pepper. Pour the apple cider into the pan. Cover the pan with aluminum foil and bake for 3–3 1/2 hours. Occasionally baste the pork with the pan juices.

Remove from the oven and let cool for about 10 minutes. Then use 2 forks to pull the pork into shreds. Mix the pulled pork with the juices, and let the meat absorb them. Drizzle with your favorite barbeque sauce and toss to combine. Serve topped with coleslaw on Kaiser rolls.

TANGY FARMHOUSE COLESLAW

» SERVES 8 TO 10

This recipe comes straight from my family's farm, where maple syrup played a large part in my life. My mother adapted her grandmother's recipe for a sweet and tangy twist in this slaw. You can make this the night before your barbeque. It will last several days in the refrigerator.

1 ½ cups mayonnaise
½ cup dark maple syrup
¼ cup freshly squeezed lemon juice
¼ cup apple cider vinegar
¼ cup vegetable oil
¾ teaspoon ground nutmeg
Salt and freshly ground pepper, to taste
6 to 8 cups chopped cabbage
½ cup chopped onion
2 cups grated carrots

In a large bowl, mix together the mayonnaise, maple syrup, lemon juice, vinegar, vegetable oil, nutmeg, salt, and pepper. Add the cabbage, onion, and carrots and stir with a rubber spatula, coating everything well. Refrigerate for several hours to allow the flavors to blend.

HOMESTYLE MAPLE BAKED BEANS

» SERVES 6 TO 8

Homemade baked beans are one of my fondest memories of my Grandfather Rusin. They cook for hours and fill your house with the sweet smells of molasses and maple syrup. This is good, old-fashioned cooking straight from our country kitchen.

- 1 (16-ounce) bag navy beans, soaked overnight
- 1 teaspoon baking soda
- 3/4 cup molasses
- 1/2 cup firmly packed brown sugar
- 1/2 cup dark maple syrup
- 3/4 cup ketchup
- 1/2 cup stone-ground mustard
- 1 large onion, peeled and finely chopped
- 1 large green bell pepper, finely chopped
- 8 slices hickory-smoked, thick-cut bacon, cooked and roughly chopped
- Onion powder, to taste
- Freshly ground black pepper, to taste

Preheat the oven to 350 degrees F.

Drain the water from the beans. Place the beans into a large pot and cover with fresh water. Add the baking soda and bring water to a boil over high heat. Continue to boil for 12–15 minutes, removing the foam with a large serving spoon.

Drain the beans in a colander and rinse. Transfer to a large ovenproof pot and cover with warm water. Add the molasses, brown sugar, maple syrup, ketchup, mustard, onion, bell pepper, and bacon. Season with onion powder and pepper. Cook for 4–5 hours, until the beans get really dark in color and the sauce thickens. Check periodically. If the beans dry out during the cooking process, add more water. By the end of the cooking time, the sauce should be thick and the beans soft.

VINAIGRETTE PASTA SALAD

»» SERVES 6 TO 8

This pasta salad uses light vinaigrette instead of heavy mayonnaise, which makes it a great addition to your summer picnics. Get creative and add in any vegetables you would like or even chunks of fresh mozzarella.

2 cups broccoli florets
1 cup chopped carrots
1 pound multicolored penne pasta
1 small red onion, chopped
½ green or red bell pepper, chopped
1 cup sugar snap peas
1 cup grape tomatoes, halved
½ cup sliced black olives, drained
½ cup pimiento-stuffed green olives
¾ cup prepared honey balsamic vinaigrette
¼ cup stone-ground mustard
1 teaspoon onion powder
½ teaspoon garlic powder
Salt and freshly ground black pepper, to taste

Bring a medium pot of water to a boil. Blanch the broccoli and the carrots for 2–3 minutes. Remove from boiling water and plunge into ice water to stop the cooking process; drain and set aside.

Bring a large pot of lightly salted water to a boil. Add the pasta and cook for 10–12 minutes, until al dente. Drain the pasta and rinse with cold water. Place the cooled pasta in a large bowl. Add the onion, bell pepper, snap peas, tomatoes, sliced olives, whole olives, vinaigrette, mustard, onion powder, garlic powder, salt, and pepper. Toss to combine all of the ingredients. Cover the bowl with plastic wrap and refrigerate for several hours to allow the flavors to blend.

CREAMY BACON DEVILED EGGS

»» MAKES 24 EGG HALVES

Probably one of my fondest memories of having family picnics at either of my grandmas' houses is the homemade deviled eggs—creamy, tangy, and a dash of spice, blended with mayonnaise and a touch of mustard.

- 12 large eggs
- 1 tablespoon Dijon mustard
- ¼ cup mayonnaise
- 1 teaspoon apple cider vinegar
- Salt and freshly ground black pepper, to taste
- 2 strips bacon, cooked and finely chopped
- Paprika, for garnish

Place the eggs in a medium saucepan and add enough cold water to cover. Bring to a boil over medium heat. Once the water comes to a boil, turn the heat down and simmer for 10–12 minutes. Drain the water from the pan, and then add ice water to cool the eggs. Leave the eggs in the pan to cool.

Gently crack the eggshells and roll the egg in your hand to loosen the membrane. Carefully peel the egg. Cut the cooked eggs in half lengthwise. Place the yolks in a medium bowl and use a fork to mash well. Place the egg halves onto a plate and set aside.

Mix the mustard, mayonnaise, vinegar, salt, and pepper with the mashed egg yolks. Spoon the egg yolk mixture into a pastry bag and use scissors to snip off the end. Pipe the smooth egg yolks evenly into the egg halves. Sprinkle with a dusting of paprika and the crumbled bacon. Cover with plastic wrap and refrigerate until ready to serve.

CHIPOTLE BACON BURGERS

»» MAKES 6 TO 8 BURGERS

My family loves homemade burgers, and this one is a favorite. Oftentimes I'll make extra burgers and place the uncooked patties between layers of wax paper, put them into a freezer-proof bag, and freeze for a quick dinner on busy nights.

- 2 pounds ground beef (80–85 percent lean)
- ½ pound smoked bacon, cooked and chopped
- 2 tablespoons diced canned chipotle peppers
- ¼ cup prepared steak sauce
- 1 teaspoon onion powder
- ½ teaspoon garlic powder
- Salt and freshly ground black pepper, to taste
- Cheese, for serving
- 6 to 8 buns, for serving
- 2 tablespoons melted butter
- Fixings (such as lettuce, tomatoes, etc.), for serving

In a medium bowl, use your hands to combine the ground beef, bacon, chipotle peppers, steak sauce, onion powder, garlic powder, salt, and pepper. Press the mixture into patties using a burger press or your hands. With your finger, press a shallow dimple into the top of each burger. This helps prevent the burgers from shrinking while they cook.

Cook the burgers over medium-high heat in a grill pan or on a grill. Cook for 3–4 minutes on each side, until burgers reach your preferred level of doneness. Place your favorite cheese on top of each burger to melt. Brush buns with butter, and toast them on the grill for a few minutes. Top burgers with your favorite fixings.

BOURBON-GLAZED SHORT RIBS

» SERVES 6 TO 8

These ribs are old-fashioned goodness for a wonderful weekend supper. The tender meat will fall right off the bone and pairs perfectly with creamy mashed potatoes.

8 slices hickory-smoked bacon, chopped

2 tablespoons olive oil

3 to 4 pounds beef short ribs

1 large onion, sliced

Salt and freshly ground black pepper, to taste

1/4 cup all-purpose flour

1 1/2 cups bourbon

1 cup apple cider

1 cup beef broth

1 tablespoon tomato paste

3 tablespoons molasses

1/4 cup stone-ground mustard

1/4 cup pure maple syrup

1/2 teaspoon smoked paprika

1 teaspoon onion powder

1 teaspoon garlic powder

Mashed potatoes, for serving

In a 6- to 8-quart enameled cast iron Dutch oven, sauté the bacon in the olive oil over medium heat. Once lightly browned, remove with a slotted spoon and set aside.

Pat the beef dry with paper towels, as it will not brown properly if it is wet. Sauté a few ribs at a time in the hot oil and bacon fat until they are evenly browned. Remove the ribs and set aside. Brown the onion in the fat. Drain the cooking fat using a large spoon.

Preheat the oven to 325 degrees F.

Return the beef and bacon to the Dutch oven and season with salt and pepper. Over medium-high heat, sprinkle the beef with flour and stir with a wooden spoon to evenly coat. Cook for about 5 minutes to lightly brown the flour. Stir in the bourbon, apple cider, and broth so the meat is just barely covered. Add the tomato paste, molasses, mustard, maple syrup, paprika, onion powder, and garlic powder. Bring to a simmer, cover the Dutch oven, and place in the middle of the oven for 2 1/2–3 hours, until the meat is tender.

Remove from the oven and skim off any excess fat. Serve over mashed potatoes.

BERRY-PEACH COBBLER

» SERVES 6 TO 8

This cobbler with a biscuit-style topping offers a sweet and tart ending to a summer meal. Top it with vanilla ice cream for even more flavor. Adjust the sugar depending on how naturally sweet the fruit is.

FILLING

3 cups fresh blackberries

2 cups fresh blueberries

6 large peaches, peeled and sliced

1/4 cup instant tapioca

1/4 to 1/2 cup granulated sugar

1/4 cup granulated maple sugar

3 tablespoons freshly squeezed lemon juice

1/2 teaspoon ground cinnamon

1/2 teaspoon ground nutmeg

TOPPING

2 cups all-purpose flour

1 1/2 teaspoons baking powder

1/2 cup granulated sugar

1/2 teaspoon kosher salt

1/2 cup (1 stick) unsalted butter, cold

1 cup buttermilk

1 teaspoon pure vanilla extract

1 large egg, lightly beaten

Vanilla ice cream, for serving

Preheat the oven to 375 degrees F. Spray a 9 x 13-inch baking pan with cooking spray, or brush with softened butter.

FILLING Toss together the blackberries, blueberries, peaches, tapioca, granulated sugar, maple sugar, lemon juice, cinnamon, and nutmeg in a large bowl. Pour the mixture into the baking pan.

TOPPING Combine the flour, baking powder, sugar, and salt in a mixing bowl. Cut in the butter using two forks or a pastry cutter until the mixture resembles coarse cornmeal. Gradually stir in the buttermilk, vanilla, and egg. Spoon the batter over the filling as evenly as you can, leaving only a few small holes.

Bake for 35–40 minutes, until the crust is golden brown and the fruit is bubbling. Let cool slightly before serving with vanilla ice cream, if desired.

FARMER'S DAUGHTER
STOCKING THE PANTRY

AS CHILDREN, WE WERE TAUGHT TO COOK, BAKE, CAN, AND CLEAN UP AFTER OURSELVES. We were not really given an option—you helped on the farm with chores and tasks. You certainly never complained, or you would be given more chores. You clean up after you are done, leaving a clean workspace behind for the next person. We were groomed as youngsters to become independent and think of others, always. We were taught to put tremendous effort into any task at hand. Hard work, sweat, and love helped us achieve goals and made us the individuals we are today.

I clearly remember the beautiful array of homemade canned goods stocked each season in the farm's stone cellar. The stone cellar was cool, and there we stored all of the year's harvest. When it was time to process apples, tomatoes, or other vegetables we harvested, we worked on our brick-red wooden picnic table under an open-air patio area that had a covered roof, electricity, and a concrete floor. Cleanup was relatively easy, as we could wash the area with a garden hose. Having an abundance of tomatoes and apples to process, we utilized a food mill called a Squeezo. The stainless-steel food mill made canning tomatoes and applesauce a breeze—no peeling or coring necessary. Juices and pulp from the fruit come out on the drain tray, while seeds and skins get discarded into separate bowl. You can also find smaller, less expensive food mills that turn with a handle.

At that same picnic table, my dad cured hams and bacon before smoking them in my grandfather's cloudy-gray smokehouse. Metal racks would hold hefty slabs of bacon, hams, and homemade sausage. Spending quality time with our mom and dad gave us

the opportunity to talk about our daily activities and to gain an enormous amount of knowledge. Often working late into the night in our outdoor patio area, we could watch fireflies dance in the peaceful country night and hear the crickets chirping.

Today a heavy-duty, commercial stainless-steel rack housed in our garage holds spare cases of canning equipment, jars, and lids. Canning pickles, jams, jellies, and sauces is not difficult and doesn't require fancy gadgets. I use a few oversized pots, jelly jars, heatproof gloves, and a ladle. It's not far from the way my grandmother and great-grandmother did things, and that's fine with me. One of my secrets behind making homemade jams and jellies is using Pomona's Pectin (pomonaspectin.com). This fruit pectin requires very little sugar to make it gel and gives you a flawless result.

When we moved to North Carolina, I was so overjoyed at the extended growing season and having an oversized vegetable garden. Last summer, I started a new vegetable garden on our property. I added six pickup-truckloads of aged horse manure and got tilling. During my first cookbook tour, I traveled often. The weeks I was home, I would harvest pickling cucumbers and make homemade pickles. On the weeks I traveled, our neighbor, Mr. Slaughter, would pick all the vegetables and make pickles and marinara sauce. Keeping the garden maintained was crucial, and his harvesting while I was gone helped me tremendously. It also made him a very happy man.

On Fridays, I'm typically baking all day long, and I'll often see Mr. Slaughter through my kitchen window, mowing our lawn. He knows that I'm crazy busy on Fridays prepping for the farmers market the following day. This small act of kindness is extremely helpful to me and our family. To repay him, I'll often bring him home a bag of freshly picked salad greens, eggs, or a vegetable or fruit I know he might need and doesn't grow himself. He also gets to taste test anything his little heart desires; I swear he can smell cookies baking a mile away.

CANNING ESSENTIALS

Measuring cups for dry ingredients (stock several sets)

Measuring cups for liquids (stock an assortment of sizes)

Measuring spoons (stock several sets)

Digital thermometer with probe (helps ensure proper temperatures)

Water bath canner (an enamel pot and lid that comes with a chrome-plated rack and canning utensils)

Glass canning jars and lids (stock various sizes for jams, jellies, pickles, and sauces)

Wide-mouth funnel (helps get your preserves neatly into jars)

Stainless-steel ladles (keep various sizes for different projects)

Rubber-tipped tongs (helps easily grip jars when canning)

Heatproof gloves (protects your hands when handling hot jars)

Pectin (to make jams and jellies gel)

GRAPE-APPLE JELLY

» MAKES 12 (8-OUNCE) JARS

My kids love this jelly on toast and for good old-fashioned peanut butter and jelly sandwiches. Keep it simple by using unsweetened bottled juice, or use a jelly bag to make juice from freshly harvested fruit.

- 5 cups grape juice
- 4 cups apple juice
- 4 cups granulated sugar, divided
- 1 (1.75-ounce) package fruit pectin
- ¼ cup freshly squeezed lemon juice

Prepare a boiling water canner. Heat the jars and lids in simmering water until ready for use. Do not boil. Set bands aside.

In an 8- to 10-quart saucepan over medium-high heat, bring the grape and apple juices to a simmer.

In a large measuring cup, combine 2 cups of the sugar with the pectin. Add the lemon juice and sugar-pectin mixture to the simmering juices. Over high heat, bring the mixture to a full rolling boil that cannot be stirred down, stirring frequently with a wooden spoon. Boil for 1 minute. Add the remaining sugar immediately, and bring back up to a hard boil for 1 to 2 minutes, stirring constantly. Reduce the heat to low to keep the jelly warm.

Ladle hot jelly into hot jars, leaving ½-inch headspace. Wipe the rims with a clean, damp paper towel. Center the lids on the jars. Apply the bands until the fit is fingertip tight. Process jars in the boiling water canner for 10 minutes, adjusting for altitude. Remove the jars and allow to cool. Check the lids for seal after 24 hours. The lid should not flex up and down when the center is pressed. Store jars in a cool, dry place. If a jar doesn't seal, store in the refrigerator and use within 4–6 weeks.

MAPLE FARMHOUSE APPLESAUCE

»» MAKES ABOUT 12 (16-OUNCE) JARS

Flavors of local apples and pure maple syrup are whisked together for a taste of autumn. There's no need to peel or core the apples, because the skin provides nutrients. Use a mixture of several different varieties of apples for the most flavor.

- 6 pounds baking apples (such as Macoun, McIntosh, Honeycrisp, or Braeburn)
- 1 ½ cups water
- ¾ cup pure maple syrup
- ¼ cup firmly packed brown sugar
- 1 teaspoon ground cinnamon
- ¼ teaspoon ground nutmeg
- ¼ teaspoon ground cloves

Wash the apples and cut into eighths. Do not peel or core. Put the apples and water into a large pot over medium heat and cover. Bring to a boil then reduce to a simmer. Let the apples simmer over low heat for 30–40 minutes, until the skins soften and fall off, stirring occasionally with a wooden spoon to prevent the apples from sticking and burning.

Remove the pot from the heat and let cool slightly. Put apples through a sieve or food mill set over a large bowl to remove the skins and seeds from the sauce. Discard the peels and seeds and return the sauce to the pot. Add the maple syrup, brown sugar, cinnamon, nutmeg, and cloves; stir thoroughly. Place the pot back over low to medium heat and simmer for 20 minutes, or until sauce reaches desired thickness. Meanwhile, prepare a boiling water canner. Heat the jars and lids in simmering water until ready for use. Do not boil. Set bands aside.

Ladle hot applesauce into hot jars, leaving ½-inch headspace. Wipe the rims with a clean, damp paper towel. Center the lids on the jars. Apply the bands until the fit is fingertip tight. Process jars in the boiling water canner for 15 minutes, adjusting for altitude. Remove the jars and allow them to cool. Check the lids for seal after 24 hours. The lid should not flex up and down when the center is pressed. Store jars in a cool, dry place. If a jar doesn't seal, store in the refrigerator and use within 4–6 weeks.

SPICED APPLE JAM

»» MAKES 12 (8-OUNCE) JARS

This is one of the most flavorful seasonal jams we make on the farm. With cinnamon, nutmeg, and brown sugar, it is the essence of autumn in a jar. It's delicious on a homemade biscuit, a slice of freshly baked bread, or a flaky croissant.

- 8 cups peeled, cored, and chopped baking apples (such as Macoun, McIntosh, Honeycrisp, or Braeburn)
- 1 cup water
- 2 cups granulated sugar
- 1 (1.75-ounce) package fruit pectin
- ¼ cup freshly squeezed lemon juice
- 2 cups firmly packed brown sugar
- 1 teaspoon ground cinnamon
- ½ teaspoon ground nutmeg

Place the apples and water in an 8- to 10-quart saucepan over low to medium heat and cover. Simmer until the apples are soft, stirring occasionally with a wooden spoon to prevent scorching. Once the apples are soft, lightly smash them with a potato masher. Meanwhile, prepare a boiling water canner. Heat the jars and lids in simmering water until ready for use. Do not boil. Set bands aside.

In a large measuring cup, combine the granulated sugar with the pectin. Add the lemon juice and sugar-pectin mixture to the apples. Over high heat, bring the mixture to a full rolling boil that cannot be stirred down, stirring frequently with a wooden spoon. Boil for 1 minute. Immediately stir in the brown sugar, cinnamon, and nutmeg. Bring back up to a hard boil for 1 minute, stirring constantly. Turn the heat to low to keep the jam warm.

Ladle hot jam into hot jars, leaving ½-inch headspace. Wipe the rims with a clean, damp paper towel. Center the lids on the jars. Apply the bands until the fit is fingertip tight. Process jars in the boiling water canner for 10 minutes, adjusting for altitude. Remove the jars and allow to cool. Check the lids for seal after 24 hours. The lid should not flex up and down when the center is pressed. Store jars in a cool, dry place. If a jar doesn't seal, store in the refrigerator and use within 4–6 weeks.

BLUEBERRY-LAVENDER JAM

» MAKES 8 (8-OUNCE) JARS

Fragrant lavender buds and bright blueberries are sinfully good together. It's a flavor combination that will surprise your friends. Be sure to purchase lavender labeled for culinary use, meaning that it hasn't been sprayed with chemicals while growing.

3 tablespoons dried lavender buds

1/2 cup water, boiling

8 cups fresh blueberries

5 cups granulated sugar, divided

1 (1.75-ounce) package fruit pectin

3 tablespoons freshly squeezed lemon juice

*Granulated vegetable defoamer can be purchased from most maple syrup equipment suppliers. This product helps eliminate foam from your jams, jellies, and preserves but does not add dairy contamination as using butter will.

Put the lavender buds in a glass measuring cup and pour the boiling water over them. Let steep for 10–15 minutes. Strain the buds, keeping the liquid and discarding the solids.

Pour the lavender infusion into a 6- to 8-quart saucepan and add the blueberries. Simmer the mixture on low to medium heat until the blueberries are soft, about 15–20 minutes. Lightly smash the berries with a potato masher. Meanwhile, prepare a boiling water canner. Heat the jars and lids in simmering water until ready for use. Do not boil. Set bands aside.

In a large measuring cup, combine 2 cups of the sugar with the pectin. Add the lemon juice and sugar-pectin mixture to the berries. Over high heat, bring the mixture to a full rolling boil that cannot be stirred down, stirring frequently with a wooden spoon. Boil for 1 minute. Add the remaining 3 cups sugar immediately and bring back to a full boil for 1 minute, stirring constantly. Turn the heat to low to keep the jam warm. Skim foam if necessary. (You can use a granulated vegetable defoamer,* if needed, to help eliminate any foam.)

Ladle hot jam into hot jars, leaving 1/2-inch headspace. Wipe the rims with a clean, damp paper towel. Center the lids on the jars. Apply the bands until the fit is fingertip tight. Process jars in the boiling water canner for 10 minutes, adjusting for altitude. Remove the jars and allow to cool. Check the lids for seal after 24 hours. The lid should not flex up and down when the center is pressed. Store jars in a cool, dry place. If a jar doesn't seal, store in the refrigerator and use within 4–6 weeks.

Ball

BLUEBERRY-PEACH PRESERVES

» MAKES 12 (8-OUNCE) JARS

Plump, juicy blueberries are married with sweet peaches to create a very flavorful preserve. Most of the peaches will melt and dissolve as this concoction cooks.

6 cups fresh blueberries

4 cups peeled and sliced peaches

5 cups granulated sugar, divided

1 (1.75-ounce) package fruit pectin

1/4 cup freshly squeezed lemon juice

*Granulated vegetable defoamer can be purchased from most maple syrup equipment suppliers. This product helps eliminate foam from your jams, jellies, and preserves but does not add dairy contamination as using butter will.

In a 6- to 8-quart saucepan over low to medium heat, cook the blueberries and peaches until soft. Lightly smash the fruit with a potato masher. Meanwhile, prepare a boiling water bath canner. Heat the jars and lids in simmering water until ready for use. Do not boil. Set bands aside.

In a large measuring cup, combine 2 cups of the sugar with the pectin. Add the lemon juice and sugar-pectin mixture to the fruit. Over high heat, bring the mixture to a full rolling boil that cannot be stirred down, stirring frequently with a wooden spoon. Boil for 1 minute. Add the remaining 3 cups sugar immediately, and bring back to a full boil for 1 minute, stirring constantly. Turn the heat to low to keep the jam warm. Skim foam if necessary. (You can use a granulated vegetable defoamer,* if needed, to help eliminate any foam.)

Ladle hot preserves into hot jars, leaving 1/2-inch headspace. Wipe the rims with a clean, damp paper towel. Center the lids on the jars. Apply the bands until the fit is fingertip tight. Process jars in the boiling water canner for 10 minutes, adjusting for altitude. Remove the jars and allow to cool. Check the lids for seal after 24 hours. The lid should not flex up and down when the center is pressed. Store jars in a cool, dry place. If a jar doesn't seal, store in the refrigerator and use within 4–6 weeks.

FARMHOUSE BREAD-AND-BUTTER PICKLES

MAKES 12 (16-OUNCE) JARS

My mother kept a vintage stoneware crock in the basement of our farmhouse—a symbol of how deep the love of pickles goes in my family. This recipe comes from my maternal great-grandmother's farm kitchen, and I hope you love it just as much as we do.

25 to 30 pickling cucumbers, sliced ¼ inch thick

½ cup pickling or kosher salt

1 large onion, diced

1 large green bell pepper, diced

1 large red bell pepper, diced

7 cups white vinegar

6 cups granulated sugar

½ teaspoon ground cloves

1 tablespoon mustard seeds

2 teaspoons celery seeds

1 ½ teaspoons turmeric

In a 5-gallon food-grade bucket, combine the sliced cucumbers, salt, onion, and the green and red bell peppers. Stir so the salt is evenly distributed. Cover the cucumber mixture with a clean kitchen towel, and place a few inches of ice on top of the towel. Allow to sit for 3–4 hours in a cool place.

Drain the vegetables and set aside. Make the brine by bringing the vinegar, sugar, cloves, mustard seeds, celery seeds, and turmeric to a boil in a large pot over high heat. Meanwhile, prepare a boiling water canner. Heat the jars and lids in simmering water until ready for use. Do not boil. Set bands aside.

Place an equal amount of cucumbers, onions, and bell peppers into each hot jar. Using a wide-mouth funnel, ladle hot pickling liquid over top of the cucumbers, leaving ½-inch headspace. Remove any air bubbles. Wipe the rims with a clean, damp paper towel. Center the lids on the jars. Apply the bands until the fit is fingertip tight. Process jars in the boiling water canner for 10 minutes, adjusting for altitude. Remove the jars and allow to cool completely on the counter for 24 hours. Check the lids for seal. The lid should not flex up and down when the center is pressed. For best flavor, let stand for 3–4 weeks before enjoying. Store the jars in a cool, dry place for up to 1 year. If a jar doesn't seal, store in the refrigerator and use within 3 months.

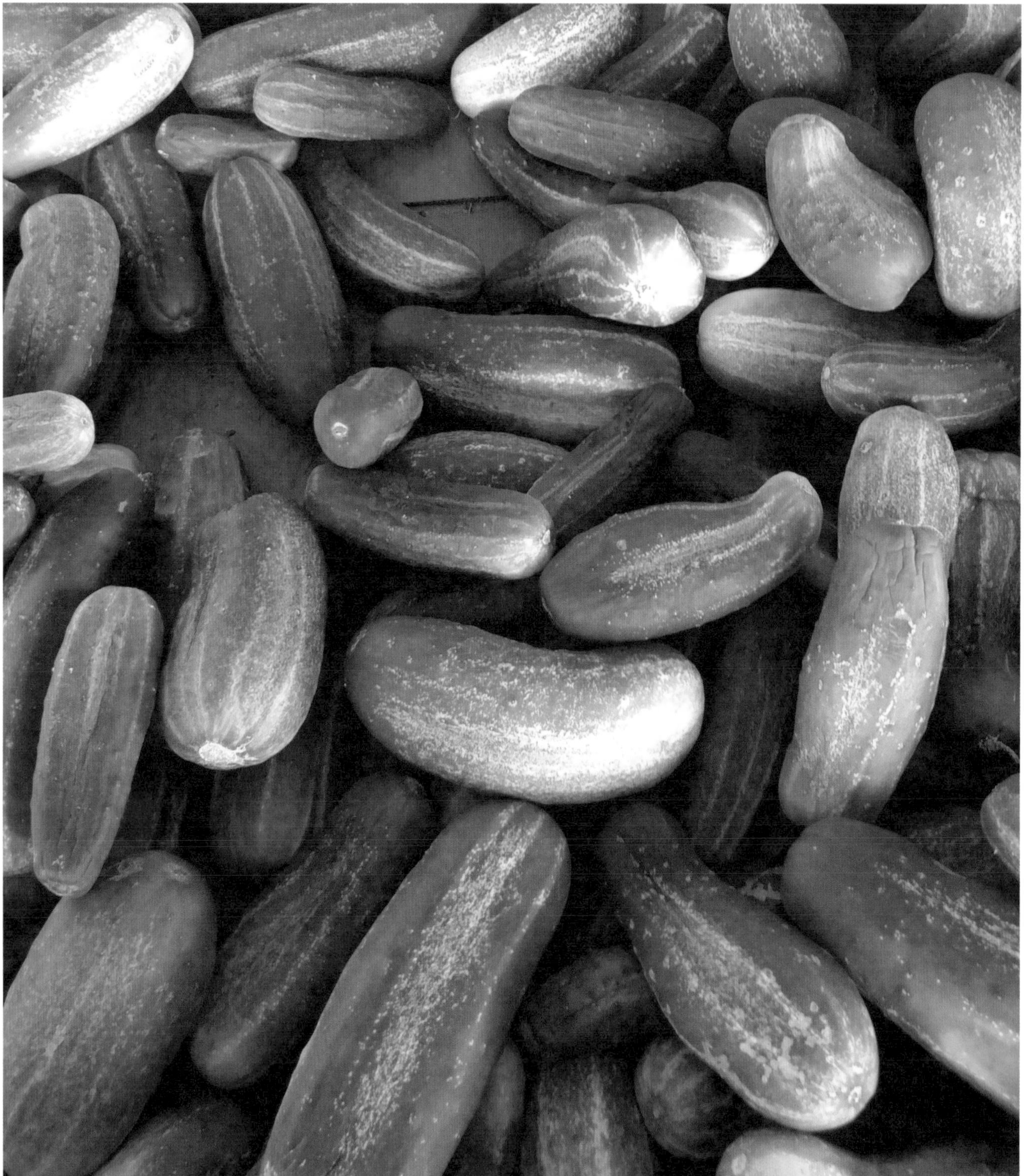

DILL PICKLES

» MAKES ABOUT 7 (16-OUNCE) JARS

What's a deli sandwich without a dill pickle? These are just like the ones Grandma used to make, bringing back memories of summer canning. Here's a tip: prep the pickles at night and can them first thing in the morning.

8 pounds pickling cucumbers, quartered

1 ¼ cups pickling or kosher salt, divided

12 cups water, divided

3 tablespoons pickling spice

6 cups white vinegar

½ cup granulated sugar

7 teaspoons mustard seeds

7 cloves garlic

10 ½ fresh dill heads, or 7 tablespoons dill seeds

Place the quartered cucumbers in a 5-gallon food-grade bucket. Dissolve ½ cup of salt in 4 cups of cold water. Pour over the cucumbers. Cover the cucumbers with a clean kitchen towel, and place several inches of ice on top of the towel. Refrigerate or store in a cool place for 10–12 hours.

When you are ready to can the pickles, prepare a boiling water canner. Heat the jars and lids in simmering water until ready for use. Do not boil. Set bands aside. Use kitchen twine to tie the pickling spice in a square of cheesecloth.

Make the brine by combining the remaining 8 cups water, vinegar, sugar, remaining ¾ cup salt, and spice bag in a large pot. Bring to a boil over medium to high heat. Stir to dissolve salt and sugar. Reduce heat and simmer for about 15 minutes.

Drain the cucumbers, rinse with cool water, and drain again thoroughly. Divide the cucumbers evenly among each jar. Into each hot jar, add 1 teaspoon mustard seeds, 1 clove garlic, and 1 ½ dill heads. Using a wide-mouth funnel, ladle hot pickling liquid over top of the cucumbers, leaving ½-inch headspace. Remove any air bubbles. Wipe the rims with a clean, damp paper towel. Center the lids on the jars. Apply the bands until the fit is fingertip tight. Process jars in the boiling water canner for 10 minutes, adjusting for altitude Remove from the water bath. Allow to cool completely on the counter for 24 hours. Check the lids for seal. The lid should not flex up and down when the center is pressed. For best flavor, let stand for 3–4 weeks before enjoying. Store the jars in a cool, dry place for up to 1 year. If a jar doesn't seal, store in the refrigerator and use within 3 months.

FARMHOUSE SWEET PICKLE RELISH

» MAKES 10 TO 12 (16-OUNCE) JARS

This sweet-and-sour relish is the perfect condiment on cheeseburgers, sausage burgers, hot dogs, and brats. If you don't grow your own bell peppers, watch farmers markets midsummer for good prices.

8 cups diced pickling cucumbers
4 cups diced green bell peppers
4 cups diced red bell peppers
2 cups diced onions
½ cup pickling or kosher salt
5 cups white vinegar
1 cup apple cider vinegar
2 ½ cups granulated sugar
2 tablespoons mustard seeds
1 tablespoon celery seeds
¼ teaspoon turmeric
⅛ teaspoon ground cloves

In a 5-gallon food-grade bucket, combine the cucumbers, green and red bell peppers, onions, and salt. Stir so the salt is evenly distributed. Cover the cucumber mixture with a clean kitchen towel, and place several inches of ice on top of the towel. Allow to sit for 3–4 hours in a cool place.

Drain the relish mixture, rinse with cool water, and drain again thoroughly. Use your hands to squeeze out any excess liquid.

Make the brine for the relish by bringing the white and apple cider vinegars, sugar, and spices to a boil in a large pot over high heat. Add the drained relish mixture and let simmer for 10–15 minutes. Meanwhile, prepare a boiling water canner. Heat the jars and lids in simmering water until ready for use. Do not boil. Set bands aside.

Using a wide-mouth funnel, carefully ladle hot relish into jars, leaving ½-inch headspace. Remove ant air bubbles. Wipe the rims with a clean, damp paper towel. Center the lids on the jars. Apply the bands until the fit is fingertip tight. Process jars in the boiling water canner for 10 minutes, adjusting for altitude Remove from the water bath. Allow to cool completely on the counter for 24 hours. Check the lids for seal. The lid should not flex up and down when the center is pressed. For best flavor, let stand for 3–4 weeks before enjoying. Store the jars in a cool, dry place for up to 1 year.

MANGO BARBEQUE SAUCE

MAKES ABOUT 3 CUPS

Homemade barbeque sauce is super easy to make. The addition of mango gives it a sweet, tropical, and tangy flavor with a kick of spice. Brush this sticky concoction on country-style ribs, grilled pork chops, or chicken.

1 cup cubed mango
1 cup molasses
½ cup firmly packed brown sugar
1 cup honey
½ cup granulated sugar
1 cup apple cider vinegar
½ cup water
¾ cup tomato paste
¼ teaspoon freshly ground black pepper
¼ teaspoon kosher salt
¼ teaspoon cayenne pepper
¼ teaspoon paprika
1 tablespoon onion powder
1 teaspoon garlic powder

*Granulated vegetable defoamer can be purchased from most maple syrup equipment suppliers.

In a medium saucepan, combine all of the ingredients and cook over medium heat, whisking to dissolve any lumps. Cook until the mango pieces have softened and the sauce has thickened to desired consistency, about 20 minutes. Use a vegetable defoamer* to eliminate any foam. To check thickness, transfer a small amount to a small cup and place in the freezer until cool. Continue cooking if the sauce needs to thicken more. Transfer the sauce into a glass jar and refrigerate for up to 4 weeks. Alternatively, process the jar in a water bath to make shelf stable.

PINK LEMONADE
A SPARKLING SUMMER JUBILEE

SUMMERS WERE VERY BUSY FOR US ON MY FAMILY'S FARM. On weekends we rushed to load pigs in the livestock trailer and haul them to country fairs throughout Connecticut. Nearly every time we needed to load pigs, it rained, making the process quite interesting. In addition to the pigs, we brought a truck full of maple products and jams to sell, along with tables, chairs, and a tent. As soon as I was done showing pigs, I changed out of show clothes and helped at the family's booth.

I also spent my summers rounding up pigs that had gotten loose and taken off through the neighborhood. We were constantly repairing fences and chasing pigs. My dad was welding in his workshop one day, and out of the side of his welding helmet, he saw something quickly run by. About a dozen mud-covered pigs were headed down our neighbor's driveway, just as she was sweeping her porch. Her front door was open, pristine white carpet exposed, and she rushed them back home frantically. But not before their snouts tore up her bubble gum–colored petunias!

Aside from the work, our summers were filled with plenty of fun. Days were spent outside, running around barefoot, swimming, and riding bicycles, not inside playing video games or watching television. I knew better than to ever say I was bored, because if I did, believe me, Daddy or Mama would surely give me something to do.

My summers are a little different now. There are no pigs to worry about, but my family and I stay busy caring for the farm and going to farmers markets on Saturdays. On Saturday nights, we eat dinner outside on the patio, sipping sweet berry wine and watching the horses graze. Heavenly aromas from the grill drift in the breeze. Sharing a home-cooked meal together at the end of the day is one of the treasures of my life. The menu is never the same; it depends on what fresh things I found that week at the market. But my family does have a few favorites that appear again and again.

BLUEBERRY-PECAN SALAD

»» SERVES 2

This is one of the tastiest summer salads I've had. Throw in a few slices of strawberries for even more flavor.

2 cups loosely packed baby greens

Thinly sliced red onion, to taste

5 to 6 grape tomatoes, halved

½ cup fresh blueberries

3 tablespoons candied pecans

2 to 3 tablespoons balsamic vinaigrette

1 boneless, skinless chicken breast, grilled and sliced

¼ cup crumbled blue cheese

Make the salad by tossing together the greens, onion, tomatoes, blueberries, pecans, and vinaigrette in a large bowl. Arrange the chicken on top of the salad and sprinkle all over with blue cheese.

CRANBERRY-WALNUT CHICKEN SALAD

»» SERVES 4 TO 6

This chicken salad is one of my favorites. It's incredible tasty on homemade multigrain bread or in a wrap.

4 boneless, skinless chicken breasts

Salt and freshly ground black pepper, to taste

2 to 3 tablespoons olive oil

2 tablespoons unsalted butter

¾ cup mayonnaise

2 tablespoons balsamic vinegar

½ small onion, finely chopped

¼ cup finely chopped celery

1 cup walnuts, chopped

1 cup dried cranberries

1 tablespoon finely chopped fresh parsley

1 tablespoon freshly squeezed lemon juice

Season the chicken with salt and pepper. In a large skillet, heat the olive oil and butter over medium heat. Cook the chicken in the pan for about 3–4 minutes on each side. Let cool slightly before chopping into chunks. Toss chicken with the mayonnaise, balsamic vinegar, onion, celery, walnuts, cranberries, parsley, and lemon juice until thoroughly combined. Refrigerate for 1 hour before serving.

HEIRLOOM TOMATO BRUSCHETTA

SERVES 4 TO 6

This traditional Italian-style appetizer is wonderful with freshly harvested heirloom tomatoes and a glass of local blush wine. Sometimes we even serve this as a light dinner with a garden salad during the summer. Use whatever tomatoes are in season.

- 4 to 5 large heirloom tomatoes, diced
- ½ cup roasted red peppers, chopped
- 1 small red onion, diced
- 2 cloves garlic, finely chopped
- Fresh basil, to taste
- ¼ cup extra virgin olive oil
- 1 tablespoon honey
- 3 tablespoons balsamic vinegar
- Salt and freshly ground black pepper, to taste
- 1 French baguette, cut into ½-inch slices
- Freshly grated or shaved Parmigiano-Reggiano cheese, to taste

In a medium bowl, toss the tomatoes, peppers, onion, garlic, and basil with olive oil, honey, and vinegar. Season with salt and pepper. Set aside.

Drizzle each baguette generously with olive oil. In a large cast iron skillet over medium to high heat, toast the baguette slices for a few minutes on each side. Remove the toasted bread from the skillet and top with bruschetta mixture. Top with Parmigiano-Reggiano and enjoy.

LEMON CHIFFON CAKE

» MAKES 1 LARGE BUNDT CAKE OR 12 MINI BUNDT CAKES

This cake is light, fluffy, and full of lemon flavor. I love making the mini Bundt cakes so everyone can have their own individual cake.

CAKE

7 large eggs, separated, room temperature

½ teaspoon cream of tartar

½ cup (1 stick) unsalted butter, softened

1 ½ cups granulated sugar

½ teaspoon pure vanilla extract

⅓ cup freshly squeezed lemon juice

2 teaspoons pure lemon oil

½ cup whole milk

2 ½ cups all-purpose or cake flour

1 tablespoon baking powder

1 teaspoon kosher salt

LEMON SYRUP

⅔ cup granulated sugar

¼ cup water

⅓ cup freshly squeezed lemon juice

LEMON ICING

2 cups powdered sugar

1 to 2 tablespoons whole milk

2 tablespoons freshly squeezed lemon juice

Preheat the oven to 325 degrees F. Brush the Bundt pan with vegetable shortening and dust with flour. Gently tap out any access flour.

CAKE Whip the egg whites with the cream of tartar until they form firm peaks. (Before whipping, be sure your beaters are clean.) Set aside. In a large mixing bowl, cream together the butter, sugar, and vanilla. Add the egg yolks and combine. Add the lemon juice, lemon oil, and milk and mix thoroughly. Add the flour, baking powder, and salt and combine well. Gently fold the whipped egg whites into the cake batter. Pour the batter into the prepared pan. Bake 50–55 minutes for a large Bundt cake (about 25 minutes for mini Bundt pans), or until a toothpick inserted into the center comes out clean.

LEMON SYRUP Dissolve the sugar in the water and lemon juice in a small saucepan over medium heat. While the cake is still in the pan, pour the lemon syrup over the top.

LEMON ICING Combine the powdered sugar, milk, and lemon juice in a small bowl. Whisk together. Add more milk if needed for desired consistency. Set aside.

Let the cake cool in the pan for 5–10 minutes and absorb the lemon syrup. Transfer the cake to a cooling rack to cool completely. Drizzle with icing and enjoy.

STRAWBERRY-PEACH SANGRIA

» SERVES 6 TO 8

I love the flavors of sweet strawberries and summery peaches blended together in this sangria recipe. They create a very flavorful drink for any gathering.

4 cups sliced strawberries

6 large peaches, peeled and sliced

¼ cup water

1 cup simple syrup

1 (9.6-ounce) can guava nectar

1 (750 ml) bottle white wine (such as Pinot Grigio or Chardonnay)

½ cup brandy

¾ cup triple sec

1 (16-ounce) can lemon-lime soda

Sliced fresh peaches, for garnish

Ice cubes, for serving

In a medium saucepan over medium heat, soften the strawberries and peaches in the water. Once soft, press through a sieve and let the juice cool. Discard the pulp and seeds.

In a glass or plastic drink dispenser, combine the cooled fruit juice, simple syrup, guava nectar, wine, brandy, triple sec, and lemon-lime soda. Adjust the alcohol as you wish. Add the peach slices and plenty of ice.

TRIPLE BERRY SANGRIA

» SERVES 6 TO 8

I've always loved these berries together, and this sangria recipe is no exception. Sensations of summer will dance and tingle in your mouth with every single sip.

2 cups fresh whole or sliced strawberries

2 cups fresh raspberries

2 cups fresh blueberries

1 cup simple syrup

1 (750 ml) bottle white wine (such as Chardonnay or Sauvignon Blanc)

¾ cup brandy

¾ cup triple sec

2 (16-ounce) cans raspberry ginger ale

Frozen blueberries, for garnish

Frozen whole strawberries, for garnish

Ice cubes, for serving

In a medium saucepan over low to medium heat, cook the strawberries, raspberries, and blueberries until soft. Press through a sieve. Let the fruit juice cool. Discard the pulp and seeds.

In a glass or plastic drink dispenser, combine the cooled fruit juice, simple syrup, wine, brandy, triple sec, and raspberry ginger ale. Adjust the alcohol as you wish. Add the frozen blueberries, frozen strawberries, and plenty of ice.

PEACH SWEET TEA

» MAKES 1 GALLON

There's nothing better than homemade sweet tea. Add the flavor of fresh peaches and you'll be in heaven. Homemade iced tea has never been easier or more flavorful.

2 cups peeled, sliced fresh peaches
4 ½ cups water, divided
8 family-size tea bags
2 cups granulated sugar
Ice cubes
Fresh mint, for garnish

In a medium saucepan over low to medium heat, soften the peaches with ½ cup of the water. Cook until very soft. Lightly smash the fruit with a potato masher. Let the purée cool.

In a large saucepan or tea kettle, boil the remaining 4 cups water. Use a large measuring cup to brew the tea bags with the boiling water. Stir in the sugar to dissolve. Let steep for 20–30 minutes. Pour the peach purée and brewed tea into a 1-gallon pouring pitcher and add enough ice to fill it to the top. Serve with additional ice and a garnish of mint.

BLACKBERRY-RASPBERRY LEMONADE

» MAKES 1 GALLON

Wild black raspberries grew up the entire length of the driveway, intertwined with a stone wall my grandfather built on our farm, all the way to our pig barn. We picked them often during the summer and froze them. I love growing some of our own berries to use in desserts, jams, and specialty drinks like this one.

1 pint fresh blackberries
1 pint fresh raspberries
3 ½ cups water, divided
2 ½ cups granulated sugar
2 cups freshly squeezed lemon juice
Fresh mint, for garnish
Ice cubes, for serving

In a medium saucepan over low to medium heat, soften the blackberries and raspberries with ½ cup of the water. Cook until very soft. Use a food mill or fine-mesh strainer to separate the juices and seeds. Let the fruit juice cool and discard the seeds and skins. In a medium saucepan, dissolve the sugar in the remaining 3 cups water, making a simple syrup.

Pour the simple syrup, lemon juice, and berry purée into a 1-gallon pouring pitcher. Add the mint leaves and plenty of ice.

Luzianne
tea

SUMMER-BERRY COCKTAIL

» SERVES 4 TO 6

This yummy and refreshing berry cocktail is perfect for summer entertaining or sipping on the patio after a long day of work in the garden. Garnish with freshly picked mint for a personalized touch.

1 pint fresh raspberries
1 pint fresh strawberries, sliced
½ cup water
½ cup granulated sugar
1 cup white rum
¼ cup freshly squeezed lime juice
¾ cup crushed ice cubes
1 (16-ounce) can lemon-lime soda
Fresh mint, for garnish

In a small saucepan over low to medium heat, combine the raspberries, strawberries, water, and sugar. Bring to a boil and stir until sugar dissolves and berries soften. Press the mixture through a sieve. Let the juice cool. Discard the pulp and seeds. In a pitcher, combine the berry juices with the rum and lime juice.

Divide the crushed ice among 4 to 6 tumblers or cocktail glasses. Pour the mixture evenly over the ice in each glass, top with lemon-lime soda, and garnish with fresh mint.

CRUSHED GRAPE SANGRIA

» SERVES 4 TO 6

This unique twist on sangria will be the hit of your next backyard barbeque. Soak in the sunset with this drink in hand; you'll thank me later.

1 cup seedless red grapes
1 cup seedless green grapes
2 cups Concord grape juice
1 cup simple syrup
½ cup brandy
½ cup white rum
1 (750 ml) bottle white wine (such as Pinot Grigio or Chardonnay)
Ice cubes, for serving
Sliced lime, for serving
Sliced oranges, for serving
Sliced red and green apples, for serving

Place the grapes in a pouring pitcher. Muddle the grapes to crush. Add the grape juice, simple syrup, brandy, rum, and wine. Add plenty of ice and stir. Garnish with lime, oranges, and apples.

FRESHLY HARVESTED
HEARTY MEALS AND HOMEMADE DESSERTS

WE WERE COMPOSTING AND RECYCLING *WAY* BEFORE IT WAS TRENDY. On the farm, we kept a five-gallon food-grade plastic "scrap" bucket in the kitchen and used an oversized metal colander to collect eggshells, coffee grounds (along with the paper filter), discarded vegetable peels, cores, bacon fat, and other leftovers. Table scraps, overgrown vegetables, and day-old bread were fed to the pigs. This effort not only kept food out of the garbage, it also kept grain costs down. Every few weeks, local dairy and bread companies would give us pickup truckloads of bread, yogurt, milk, and baked goods that were out of date. We fed these to the pigs during the fall and winter to supplement their grain diet. During the winter, we dumped woodstove ashes into the vegetable garden and tilled them into the soil in the spring. Old newspapers were crumpled up and stuffed in between kindling in the stove, along with firewood we split ourselves, which heated the house. It also fueled the evaporator in which we cooked maple syrup.

Today, I farm on a smaller scale but retain the mindset of throwing out as little as possible. We plant corn in rows, rotate crops, recycle, compost, and repair and utilize what we already have instead of buying something new. As I toss eggshells into my five-gallon bucket, I remember my grandmother adding coffee grounds and kitchen scraps to her compost bucket. We harvest varieties of tomatoes my grandfather grew and try out new heirlooms. We make our own tomato cages, just like my dad made in his workshop on our farm. I believe that some things are meant to stay the same. Rural living worked well for my parents, and their children turned out pretty good. So why not continue the same way with our children? After a hard day's work, we enjoy sitting down to a good hearty meal accompanied by a homemade dessert.

BOEUF BOURGUIGNON

SERVES 8 TO 10

This is a one-pot wonder that will simmer in the oven for hours while you do weekend chores. The savory smells of this French-style beef stew will fill your kitchen. Dip slices of crusty French baguette into the rich sauce, and your belly will be delighted.

- 8 slices bacon, chopped
- 1 tablespoon olive oil
- 3 to 3 ½ pounds stew beef
- 1 large onion, sliced
- 6 large carrots, peeled and sliced
- Salt and freshly ground black pepper, to taste
- ¼ cup all-purpose flour
- 3 cups dry red wine (such as Cabernet Sauvignon, Merlot, or Pinot Noir)
- 2 ½ to 3 cups beef stock
- 1 tablespoon tomato paste
- 3 cloves garlic, smashed
- 1 teaspoon dried parsley
- 1 teaspoon dried basil
- 2 teaspoons dried thyme
- 1 teaspoon ground mustard
- 18 to 20 pearl onions, peeled
- 1 pint baby portobella mushrooms, sliced (optional)
- Roasted Garlic Mashed Potatoes (page 102), for serving

In a 6-quart enameled cast iron Dutch oven, sauté the bacon in the olive oil over medium heat. Once lightly browned, remove with a slotted spoon and set aside.

Pat the beef dry with paper towels, as it will not brown properly if wet. Sauté a few pieces at a time in the hot oil and bacon fat until they are evenly browned. Remove the beef from the pot and set aside. Brown the onion and carrots in the fat. Drain the cooking fat.

Preheat the oven to 325 degrees F.

Return the beef and bacon to the Dutch oven and season with salt and pepper. Sprinkle the beef with flour and stir with a wooden spoon to evenly coat. Cook for about 5 minutes over medium-high heat, stirring occasionally, to lightly brown the flour. Stir in the wine and beef stock so the meat is just barely covered. Add the tomato paste, garlic, parsley, basil, thyme, and mustard. Bring to a simmer then cover.

Place the pot in the middle of the oven for 2 ½–3 hours, until the meat is tender. During the last 30 minutes of cooking, remove the lid, place the pearl onions and sliced mushrooms over the top of the stew, and put the lid back on. Remove from the oven and skim off any excess fat. Serve over mashed potatoes.

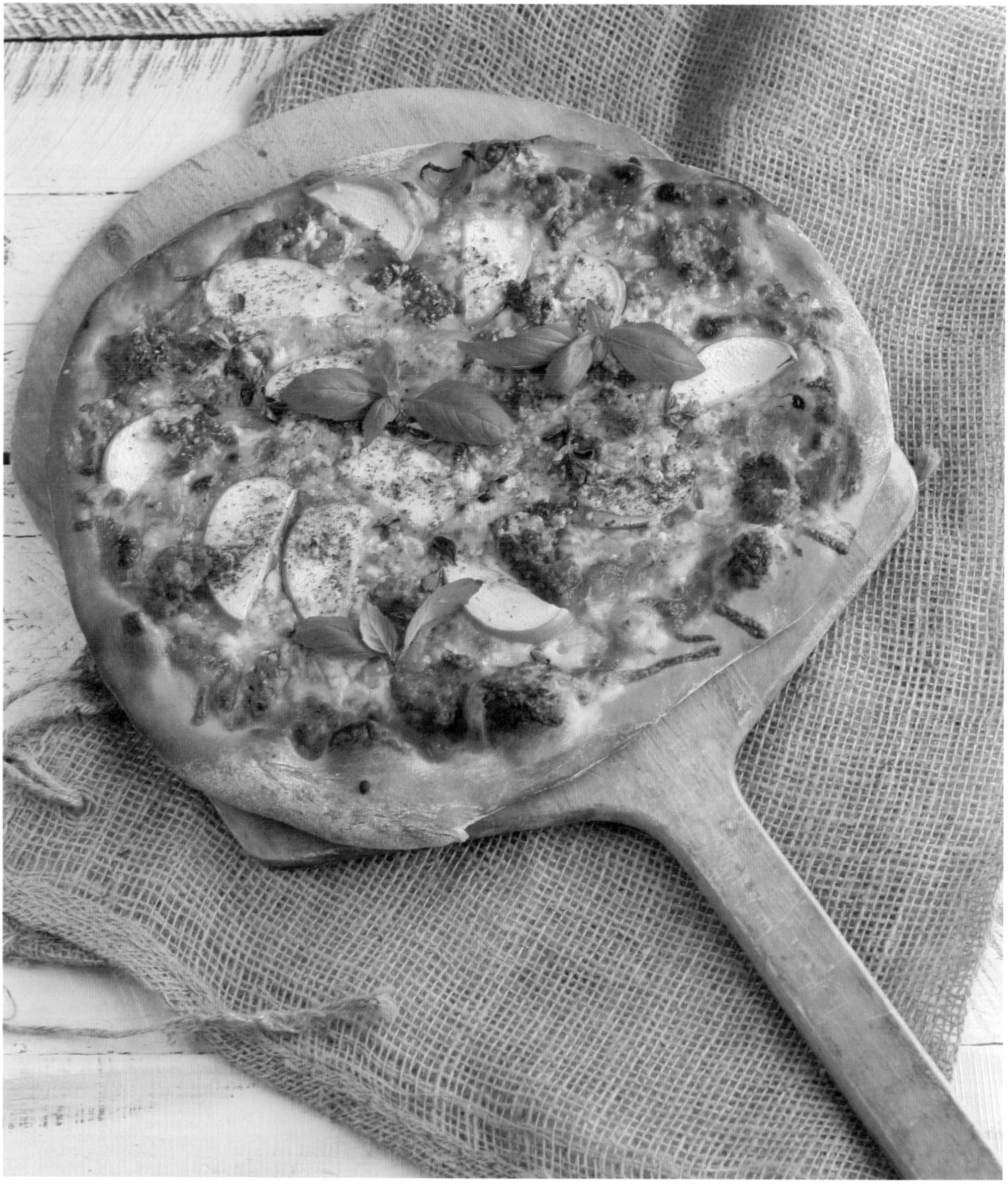

SWEET SAUSAGE AND APPLE PIZZA

» SERVES 6

Pork sausage with the tart flavor of Granny Smith apples, caramelized onions, and a touch of Gorgonzola cheese send this pizza out of this world. This recipe makes enough dough for four pizzas, so you can either store the unused dough or increase the amount of toppings and make more than one pizza.

DOUGH

- 1 (.25-ounce) packet (2 1/4 teaspoons) active dry yeast
- 1 1/2 cups water, lukewarm
- 2 tablespoons granulated sugar
- 3 tablespoons extra virgin olive oil
- 4 1/2 cups all-purpose or bread flour
- 1 teaspoon kosher salt
- Cornmeal, for dusting

TOPPINGS

- 1 tablespoon extra virgin olive oil
- 1 cup Farmhouse Marinara Sauce page 143
- 1 1/2 cups grated mozzarella or pizza-blend cheese
- 1/4 to 1/2 pound ground sweet sausage
- 1/2 Granny Smith apple, cored and thinly sliced
- 1/2 cup caramelized onions
- 1/4 cup crumbled Gorgonzola cheese
- 1 teaspoon dried oregano

DOUGH Dissolve the yeast in the water. In the bowl of a stand mixer or in a large mixing bowl, mix dissolved yeast, sugar, and olive oil with a rubber spatula or wire whisk. Attach the dough hook to the mixer and incorporate the flour and salt until dough pulls away from the sides of the bowl.

Turn dough out onto a floured work surface and knead until smooth, 5–6 minutes. Grease the mixing bowl and place the dough back in. Cover with plastic wrap and let rise in a warm area until doubled, about 1 hour. Punch down. Let rise again until doubled, about 1 hour. Turn out onto a lightly floured work surface and divide evenly into 4 rounds. Place any unused pizza dough into a plastic bag that has been sprayed with cooking spray, and then refrigerate or freeze. Dough will last for up to 2 days in the fridge and about 1 month in the freezer. Cover the rounds loosely with plastic wrap and let rise in a warm area until doubled, about 1 hour.

Place a pizza stone into the oven and preheat to 550 degrees F.

Roll out pizza dough into a 12–14-inch circle. Sprinkle a wooden pizza paddle with a few tablespoons of cornmeal. Place the rolled out dough on top. Quickly pull back and forth to ensure the pizza dough doesn't stick to the wooden paddle.

TOPPINGS Use a tablespoon to spread the olive oil on the dough, leaving 1–1 1/2 inches of crust without oil. Repeat with the marinara sauce. Pull the paddle back and forth after placing each topping, ensuring your dough does not stick. Add a light sprinkle of mozzarella, and then evenly distribute the sausage in small clumps. Add the apple, onions, Gorgonzola, and oregano. Sprinkle with the remaining mozzarella cheese. Quickly slide the uncooked pizza onto the hot pizza stone. Bake for 12–15 minutes, or until the cheese is bubbly and the crust is golden brown.

HOMESTYLE BEEF ROAST

»» SERVES 4 TO 6

With this roast, the flavors of a farm kitchen are delivered to yours. I loved when my mom made a beef roast—the way it caramelized on the outside but was pink and juicy in the center. She always made gravy to go with it.

ROAST

1 (4-pound) boneless rib-eye roast

2 tablespoons brown sugar

2 teaspoons onion powder

1 teaspoon garlic powder

1 tablespoon all-purpose flour

Salt and freshly ground black pepper, to taste

½ cup (1 stick) unsalted butter, softened

GRAVY

1 tablespoon cornstarch

1 cup water, warm

Freshly ground black pepper, to taste

2 pints baby portobella mushrooms, sliced (optional)

Preheat the oven to 450 degrees F.

ROAST Place the beef in a roasting pan, fat side up. Rub the brown sugar, onion powder, garlic powder, flour, salt, pepper, and butter over the top. Roast in the oven for about 20 minutes. Reduce the heat to 325 degrees F and continue cooking for about 1 ½ hours, until a meat thermometer inserted into the center of the roast reads 145 degrees F. Remove from the oven, cover loosely with aluminum foil, and let rest for about 10 minutes. Transfer the roast to a plate, skim off excess fat as needed, and cover with aluminum foil to keep warm.

GRAVY Mix the cornstarch with the water. Stir to remove any lumps. Skim off any excess fat from the meat juices. Pour cornstarch mixture into the roasting pan with meat juices. Cook on the stovetop over medium to high heat, whisking as you go to remove any lumps. Season with pepper. After the gravy cooks, stir in mushroom slices if desired.

BROWN SUGAR WHISKEY STEAK

»» SERVES 4 TO 6

With a sweet and tangy marinade and a topping of roasted garlic and blue cheese butter, this savory steak pairs well with a fresh garden salad and a glass of Chardonnay.

STEAK

3 tablespoons brown sugar

2 tablespoons honey

2 tablespoons stone-ground mustard

½ cup whiskey

¼ cup balsamic vinegar

¼ cup extra virgin olive oil

1 tablespoon onion powder

1 teaspoon garlic powder

1 teaspoon kosher salt

1 teaspoon freshly ground black pepper

4 to 6 T-bone, New York strip, or tenderloin steaks

GARLIC BLUE CHEESE BUTTER

6 tablespoons unsalted butter, softened

3 tablespoons crumbled blue cheese

4 cloves garlic, roasted and smashed

½ small shallot, minced

Salt and freshly ground black pepper, to taste

For the steak, combine the brown sugar, honey, mustard, whiskey, balsamic vinegar, olive oil, onion powder, garlic powder, salt, and pepper in a ziplock bag; rub everything together with your fingers on the outside of the bag. Place the steaks in the bag and let marinate in the refrigerator for 4–24 hours. When ready to cook, allow the steaks to come to room temperature while preparing the grill.

Meanwhile, for the topping, mix the butter, blue cheese, garlic, and shallot in a small bowl. Season with salt and pepper.

Grill the steaks on medium-high heat for about 6 minutes on each side, or until desired doneness is reached. Transfer steaks to a plate, cover with aluminum foil, and allow to rest for 5–10 minutes. Finish each steak with Garlic Blue Cheese Butter and serve.

ROASTED GARLIC MASHED POTATOES

» SERVES 6 TO 8

We absolutely love Boeuf Bourguignon (page 96) served on top of these rich and creamy potatoes. Roasting garlic is simple and adds depth of flavor.

- 3 heads garlic
- 2 tablespoons olive oil
- Salt and freshly ground black pepper, to taste
- 6 to 8 medium to large russet potatoes, washed, peeled, and cut into ½-inch pieces
- ½ cup (1 stick) unsalted butter, cut into pieces
- 1 cup heavy whipping cream

Preheat the oven to 400 degrees F.

Place 2 layers of aluminum foil on a baking pan. Cut off the very tops of the garlic heads, place them on the foil, drizzle with olive oil, and sprinkle with salt and pepper. Roast in the oven for 30–35 minutes. Remove from the oven and let cool slightly before handling.

While the garlic is roasting, place the potatoes in a large pot and cover with cold water. Bring to a boil over high heat and cook until tender. Drain the potatoes in a colander and return to the pot. Add the butter and cream then mash with a potato masher or electric hand mixer. Stir in salt and pepper. Squeeze roasted garlic cloves into the mashed potatoes and stir. Cover the pot to keep the mashed potatoes warm until ready to serve.

COUNTRY-STYLE MEATLOAF

» SERVES 4 TO 6

If you like old-fashioned, simple goodness, you'll love this recipe. The sauce on top keeps the meatloaf moist and caramelizes in the oven.

MEATLOAF

2 pounds ground chuck (80 percent lean)

1 pound ground sweet sausage

1/2 cup ketchup

1/4 cup prepared honey barbeque sauce

3 large eggs, lightly beaten

1 cup grated Parmesan, Asiago, and Romano cheese mixture

1 cup seasoned bread crumbs

1 medium onion, chopped

2 teaspoons onion powder

Kosher salt and freshly ground black pepper, to taste

GLAZE

1/2 cup ketchup

1/2 cup stone-ground mustard

1/4 cup honey barbeque sauce

Preheat the oven to 375 degrees F.

MEATLOAF Mix together all of the ingredients in a large bowl until well combined. Place the meat mixture into a loaf pan.

GLAZE Combine all of the ingredients in a small bowl, mix well, and spoon over top of the unbaked meatloaf.

Bake meatloaf until fully cooked, 50–55 minutes. Allow to rest for about 5 minutes before serving.

SEAFOOD AND ROASTED CORN CHOWDER

SERVES 4 TO 6

Roast summer corn on the grill, shuck it, and add it to this creamy soup. Use your favorite seafood if lobster is unavailable.

- 6 slices bacon, diced
- 1 large onion, diced
- ½ cup diced celery
- 2 cloves garlic, minced
- ½ cup (1 stick) unsalted butter
- ¼ cup all-purpose flour
- 2 cups chicken broth
- 2 large russet potatoes, peeled and cut into ½-inch cubes
- 3 cups whole milk
- 1 cup heavy whipping cream
- 1 tablespoon parsley, finely chopped
- 1 ½ cups roasted corn kernels
- 1 (7-ounce) jar roasted red peppers, drained and chopped
- 1 pound uncooked small shrimp, peeled and deveined
- Salt and freshly ground black pepper, to taste
- 1 ¼ pounds cooked lobster meat

In a large Dutch oven over medium heat, cook the bacon until browned. Add the onion and celery and cook until the onion is translucent and soft. Add the garlic and cook for a few more minutes until slightly softened. Add the butter and allow to melt. Add the flour to the pot and stir briskly with a wooden spoon. The mixture will start to thicken. Add the chicken broth and potatoes. Cook until the potatoes are soft, 20–30 minutes.

Gradually add the milk and cream to the pan while stirring briskly. The mixture will be thick and creamy. Add the parsley, corn, red peppers, and shrimp; season with salt and pepper. Turn the heat down to low and simmer gently for about 10 minutes, stirring frequently. Add the lobster meat and cook until warm, about another 10 minutes.

MAPLE-PECAN BLONDIE BARS

MAKES 18 TO 20 BARS

The flavors of New England and the South combine to create the best dessert bar you've ever tasted. Serve warm with a scoop of vanilla ice cream for a comforting dessert.

- 1 cup (2 sticks) unsalted butter, softened
- ½ cup granulated maple sugar
- 1 ½ cups firmly packed brown sugar
- 2 teaspoons pure vanilla extract
- 3 large eggs, room temperature
- 3 cups all-purpose flour
- 1 teaspoon kosher salt
- 1 ½ teaspoons baking powder
- 1 teaspoon baking soda
- ½ cup chopped pecans
- 1 cup semisweet chocolate chips

Preheat the oven to 350 degrees F. Spray a 9 x 13-inch baking pan with cooking spray and set aside.

In the bowl of a stand mixer, or in a large bowl using an electric hand mixer, cream together the butter, maple sugar, and brown sugar. Add the vanilla and eggs and combine. Add the flour, salt, baking powder, and baking soda and combine. Scrape the sides and bottom of the bowl occasionally with a rubber spatula, making sure everything is thoroughly combined. Add the pecans and chocolate chips and mix just until combined.

Spread the dough as evenly as possible in the pan. Bake for about 35 minutes, until golden brown. Let cool almost completely before cutting into squares.

HOMEMADE PIES

Flaky and bubbly homemade pies were a huge part of my childhood. On our small farm, berries, apples, and other fruits were readily available. The following recipes are for homemade crust, which is very simple to make and only requires a handful of ingredients, and a few embellished pies to inspire your own homemade creations. The sugar in the fruit pies can be adjusted based on how sweet the fruit is.

PIE CRUST

MAKES 2 (9-INCH) PIE CRUSTS

When we first moved to North Carolina I was delighted to find old-fashioned style grocery stores, butcher shops, and an abundance of farmers markets. I also fell in love when I found refined lard in a tub on the grocery store shelves! Lard makes some of the very best pie crusts.

- 2 ½ cups all-purpose flour
- 2 tablespoons granulated sugar
- 1 teaspoon kosher salt
- ⅔ cup lard
- 3 tablespoons unsalted butter, cold
- ⅓ cup water, ice cold

In a large bowl, combine the flour, sugar, and salt with a fork. Cut in the lard and butter with a pastry cutter until you have pea-size pieces. Gently combine the mixture with a little cold water. Add the remaining water and gently roll the mixture around in the bowl to combine. Do not overwork the dough or the crust will be tough. Place the pie crust in a large ziplock bag and refrigerate for 2–3 hours or overnight.

When ready to use the dough, divide into 2 portions. (If you are making a single-crust pie, wrap 1 dough portion in plastic wrap, return it to the ziplock bag, and refrigerate for up to 3 days or freeze for up to 3 months.) Turn out onto a lightly floured surface and use a rolling pin to flatten the dough. Apply even pressure, pressing your rolling pin into the dough and rolling away from you. Rotate the dough and flip it over occasionally as you work. Continue to dust with additional flour as needed. The crusts should be about 9 inches wide and ¼ inch thick. Use the crust as directed in the pie recipe.

BLUEBERRY-PEACH PIE

» MAKES 1 PIE

This is one of my favorite pies to make during the summer with fresh peaches and juicy blueberries. Adjust the amount of sugar in the recipe depending on how sweet the fruit is.

- 8 to 9 peaches, peeled and sliced
- 4 cups fresh blueberries
- 3/4 to 1 cup granulated sugar, plus more for sprinkling
- 3 tablespoons freshly squeezed lemon juice
- 1/2 cup instant tapioca
- 1/2 teaspoon ground nutmeg
- 1/4 teaspoon ground cinnamon
- 2 (9-inch) unbaked pie crusts (page 107)
- 1 large egg mixed with 1 teaspoon cold water

Place the peaches, blueberries, sugar, lemon juice, tapioca, nutmeg, and cinnamon in a large bowl. Toss with a spoon to evenly coat the fruit. Set aside.

Gently place 1 pie crust into a 9-inch pie plate. Trim the edges as needed with kitchen shears. Fill with the peach and blueberry mixture.

Preheat the oven to 400 degrees F.

Gently place the remaining pie crust on top of the entire pie. Trim the edges, if necessary. Roll the crust edges under and pinch with your fingers. Slice a few air holes in the top center of the pie. Or, if your prefer, you can create a lattice top for the pie as shown in the photograph. See page 114 for instructions. Brush with the egg wash and sprinkle with granulated sugar.

Bake for about 40 minutes. Remove pie from oven and place a piece of aluminum foil over the entire pie. Slice a hole in the center of the foil to let steam out. This will keep the pie cooking without burning or turning the crust too dark. Lower the temperature to 375 degrees F and continue baking for 20–30 minutes, until the crust is golden brown and the filling is bubbling. Let cool completely before slicing.

BLUEBERRY SKILLET PIE

» MAKES 1 PIE

Once you bake a pie in an old-fashioned cast iron skillet, there will be no turning back. The Lodge company has been manufacturing cast iron cookware in South Pittsburg, Tennessee, for over 120 years.

4 to 5 cups fresh wild blueberries (the small ones have more flavor)

1 to 1 ½ cups granulated sugar, plus more for sprinkling

2 tablespoons freshly squeezed lemon juice

⅓ cup instant tapioca

½ teaspoon ground nutmeg

1 teaspoon canola oil

2 (9-inch) unbaked pie crusts (page 107)

1 large egg mixed with 1 teaspoon cold water

Vanilla ice cream, for serving

Place the blueberries, sugar, lemon juice, tapioca, and nutmeg in a large bowl. Toss with a spoon to evenly coat the fruit. Set aside.

Using your fingers or a clean paper towel, brush the bottom and sides of a 9-inch cast iron skillet with canola oil. Gently place 1 pie crust into the skillet. Trim the edges with kitchen shears as needed. Fill with the blueberry mixture

Preheat the oven to 400 degrees F.

Gently place the remaining pie crust on top of the entire pie. Trim the edges if necessary. Roll under the crust edges and pinch with your fingers. Slice a few air holes in the top center of the pie. Brush with the egg wash and sprinkle with granulated sugar.

Bake for about 40 minutes. Remove pie from oven and place a piece of aluminum foil over the entire pie. Slice a hole in the center of the foil to let steam out. This will keep the pie cooking without burning it or turning the crust too dark. Lower the temperature to 375 degrees F and continue baking for 20–30 minutes, until the crust is golden brown and the filling is bubbling. Let cool completely before slicing and serving with a scoop of ice cream.

CHERRY PIE

» MAKES 1 PIE

Cherry pie has been a favorite in our household for many years. Making your own cherry pie filling is wonderfully simple. You will never want to use store-bought filling again.

- 4 pounds Bing cherries, pitted
- 1 to 1 ½ cups granulated sugar
- ¼ cup freshly squeezed lemon juice
- 2 tablespoons cornstarch
- ¼ cup water, warm
- 2 (9-inch) unbaked pie crusts (page 107)
- 1 large egg mixed with 1 teaspoon cold water

Pit the cherries over a glass liquid measuring cup. Place pitted cherries into a deep skillet. Place your hand over the pits and pour any excess juices into the pan.

Cook the cherries over medium heat. Add the sugar and lemon juice. Cook until soft, stirring occasionally with a wooden spoon. Dissolve the cornstarch in the water. Stir into the cherry mixture. Cook over medium to high heat to thicken, stirring constantly with a wooden spoon. Let cool completely.

Gently place 1 pie crust into a 9-inch pie plate. Trim the edges as needed with kitchen shears. Fill with the cherry mixture.

Preheat the oven to 400 degrees F.

Gently place the remaining pie crust on top of the entire pie. Trim the edges if necessary. Roll the crust edges under and pinch with your fingers. Slice a few air holes in the top center of the pie. Brush with the egg wash.

Bake for about 40 minutes. Remove pie from oven and place a piece of aluminum foil over the entire pie. Slice a hole in the center of the foil to let steam out. This will keep the pie cooking without burning it or turning the crust too dark. Lower the temperature to 375 degrees F and continue baking for 20–30 minutes, until the crust is golden brown and the filling is bubbling. Let the pie cool completely before slicing.

PEACH MEDLEY PIE

» MAKES 1 PIE

The pie crust in this recipe is slightly different than the traditional crust. Cream cheese is blended into the dough, making it more of a pastry crust and bringing a unique flavor to the pie.

CRUST

2 ½ cups all-purpose flour

1 tablespoon granulated sugar

1 teaspoon kosher salt

½ cup (1 stick) unsalted butter, cold

4 ounces cream cheese, cold

5 to 6 tablespoons water, ice cold

1 large egg mixed with 1 teaspoon cold water

Granulated sugar, for sprinkling

FILLING

5 to 6 large peaches, pitted, peeled, and sliced

2 cups fresh blueberries

2 cups fresh blackberries

1 cup fresh raspberries

1 cup granulated sugar

½ cup instant tapioca

3 tablespoons freshly squeezed lemon juice

CRUST Mix together the flour, sugar, and salt in a large bowl. Cut the butter and cream cheese into small pieces and toss them in the flour mixture. Using a pastry cutter or two forks, cut in the butter and cream cheese until you have pea-size pieces

Add ice cubes to a liquid measuring cup and then add cold water. Add a little water at a time to the flour mixture, gently tossing the mixture around until it stays together in your hand. Once it clumps together, transfer the dough to a large ziplock bag. Refrigerate the dough for a minimum of 2 hours, or overnight.

FILLING Combine the peaches, blueberries, blackberries, raspberries, sugar, tapioca, and lemon juice in a large bowl. Gently toss with a spoon and set aside.

Divide the dough into two equal pieces. Roll out one half on a floured surface. Fold it into quarters to safely lift and place into a 9-inch pie dish. Trim any excess pie dough with kitchen shears. Pour the fruit mixture into the pie crust.

Preheat the oven to 400 degrees F.

Roll out the remaining half of dough and cut into ½- to ¾-inch-wide strips using a pastry roller, small pizza cutter, or sharp knife. Place 3 to 5 strips of dough across the top of the pie. Fold back every other strip. Place a strip of dough across the unfolded strips. Unfold the folded strips across the new strip. Continue to weave the crust until the entire pie is covered. Lightly brush the entire pie with the egg wash and sprinkle with granulated sugar. Place the entire pie on a half sheet pan lined with parchment paper. This will catch any juices that drip.

Bake for 60–70 minutes, until the crust is golden brown and the fruit is bubbling. Let the pie cool completely before slicing. If the crust starts to brown too much during baking, place a piece of aluminum foil over the entire pie, and slice a hole in the center of the foil to let steam escape.

BUTTER
BUTTER

BUTTER
BUTTER

HOME BAKERY
MAKING HOMEMADE BREAD AND PASTRIES

I WILL BE THE FIRST TO ADMIT THAT HOMEMADE BREAD BAKING CAN BE A CHALLENGE. I've had my fair share of epic failures in the kitchen, making bread and cakes from scratch. I observed my mom making bread, cakes, and pastries for years and turning them into a home-based business, so I came by my entrepreneurial gene honestly. Before becoming a full-time farmer, my dad worked in the aerospace industry. Each week, he would bring a form into work for his coworkers to order my mom's homemade creations. He would deliver their goodies to smiles and delight.

When my husband, kids, and I moved to North Carolina, I discovered that farmers markets are a huge business here. I took the skills that I learned from nearly twenty years of running my own floral design business, my experience on my parents' farm, and my love of food and created a company to sell my homemade products. Ample knowledge of food safety, creative packaging, baking, and canning helped to make the process of setting up a home-based bakery and food business go smoothly. Cooking is fun, but cooking for enjoyment and making a business of it are two different entities. Here are some issues to consider if you're thinking about starting your own business:

- Know what your state requires for permits and the kitchen inspections you might need. (I researched the rules in North Carolina and met them before applying to sell at farmers markets.)
- If you have not had much commercial food processing experience, consider taking a food safety course. An acidified foods course is typically required to make things such as pickles.

- Identify locations where you could sell your products (e.g., farmers markets, fairs, etc.)
- Neat and tidy packaging is a must, along with proper labeling. Each state has different requirements. I kept my labeling simple and attractive. I handwrite product descriptions on one label that has my logo and print another with the ingredient list on mailing address labels.
- Create an eye-appealing display. Spending a little extra effort on presentation might be the difference between a customer buying from you or from another vendor. For example, if your table linens are dirty and crooked, that might suggest to the customer that you don't put effort into the products you make. Multilevel risers help display products more prominently than flat tables.
- Sampling products at the market is a fabulous way to sell more. If consumers can taste what I've made before buying it, they are more likely to make the purchase. Some states require health permits for sampling.
- Great signage will help identify your company and brand to customers passing by your stand.
- Know your market, your customer, and their needs/wants. Observe how customers shop the market or other venue you're considering. For example, at the market I attend, I would estimate that 90 percent of customers bring their own reusable bag. Since I know customers at this market are very earth conscious, I stock recycled brown paper bags for anyone who needs one. Also, I look at what products they love and don't love. I change my offerings from week to week to entice return customers and draw new ones.
- Focus on the customer. Silence your cell phone and stay off of it, unless you need to use it to charge a customer's credit card. Be polite, kind, and always smile. Stand up and greet customers when they stop by. Learn how to read customers' body language. For example, I'll often say hello to customers if they glance at my booth but will only interact with them more if they walk closer and show interest. I don't want to seem pushy or make their farmers market experience negative in any way.

POTATO ROLLS

MAKES 24 ROLLS

This is a beloved recipe from the kitchen of Mr. Bendza. I'm fortunate to have all of his handwritten and typed bread recipes. I think you'll love this one.

- 4 to 4 ½ cups all-purpose or bread flour, divided
- 1 (.25-ounce) packet (2 ¼ teaspoons) active dry yeast
- 1 cup whole milk
- ¼ cup water (from boiled potatoes)
- ¼ cup granulated sugar
- ¼ cup vegetable shortening
- 1 teaspoon kosher salt
- 1 large egg, beaten
- ½ cup mashed potatoes

In the bowl of a stand mixer, or in a large bowl using an electric hand mixer, stir together 2 cups of the flour and the yeast. In a medium saucepan over medium heat, warm the milk. Stir in the water, sugar, shortening, and salt; continue heating just until warm (120 to 130 degrees F) and the shortening almost melts. Add the milk mixture to the flour mixture along with the egg and mashed potatoes. Mix with the dough hook for about 4 minutes, adding enough of the remaining flour to make a moderately stiff dough.

Turn the dough out onto a lightly floured work surface and knead for about 6 minutes. Place the dough into a greased bowl, cover with plastic wrap, and let rise in a warm area until doubled, about 1 hour.

Line a sheet pan with parchment paper. Divide the dough into 24 portions, shape into rolls, and place on the pan. Cover loosely with plastic wrap and let rise until doubled, about 1 hour.

Preheat the oven to 400 degrees F. Bake rolls for 10–12 minutes, until golden brown. Remove rolls from the baking sheet and cool on cooling rack.

OLD-FASHIONED OATMEAL BREAD

MAKES 3 LOAVES

This recipe comes straight from the kitchen of our close family friend, Mr. Edward Bendza, in Whigville, Connecticut. He was an expert home bread baker who raised his own laying hens and kept a meticulous vegetable garden.

- 1 ¼ cups old-fashioned rolled oats, divided
- ½ cup vegetable shortening or lard
- 1 teaspoon kosher salt
- 2 cups whole milk
- 1 (.25-ounce) packet (2 ¼ teaspoons) active dry yeast
- ½ cup water, lukewarm
- ¾ cup pure maple syrup
- 2 large eggs, room temperature
- 6 cups bread flour, sifted
- 1 cup wheat germ
- 1 egg, beaten
- 1 tablespoon brown sugar

In a large bowl, combine 1 cup of the oats, shortening, and salt. In a medium saucepan, bring the milk to a gentle boil. Pour hot milk over the oat mixture. Stir, cover, and cool to lukewarm.

Dissolve the yeast in the water. In the bowl of a stand mixer, or in a large bowl using an electric hand mixer, mix the maple syrup, eggs, and dissolved yeast with the oatmeal mixture. Using the dough hook, stir in the flour and wheat germ and combine well. Turn dough out onto a lightly floured work surface and knead the bread for about 8 minutes. Place the dough into a greased bowl and cover with plastic wrap. Let rise in a warm place until doubled in size, 1–1 ½ hours.

Grease three 9 x 5-inch loaf pans and set aside. Punch dough down and shape into 3 loaves. Transfer to the prepared pans. Make a sharp cut down the center of each loaf. Brush each loaf with the beaten egg and sprinkle with the remaining ¼ cup rolled oats and brown sugar. Cover loosely with plastic wrap and let rise until doubled, 1–1 ¼ hours.

Preheat the oven to 375 degrees F. Bake loaves for 33–35 minutes, until golden brown. Let cool for 10 minutes. Remove from bread pans and let cool completely.

FARMHOUSE SOURDOUGH BREAD

» MAKES 2 LOAVES

Sourdough is one of my favorite types of bread. This bread is fairly simple to make and is quite enjoyable sliced for sandwiches or toast. Get the starter going four to six days before you plan to bake the bread. You can put the starter in the refrigerator and keep it fed for later use.

SOURDOUGH STARTER

1 (.25-ounce) packet (2 ¼ teaspoons) active dry yeast

2 ½ cups water, lukewarm

1 tablespoon granulated sugar

2 cups all-purpose flour

1 teaspoon kosher salt

BREAD

½ cup whole milk

1 tablespoon granulated sugar

1 cup water, lukewarm

1 (.25-ounce) packet (2 ¼ teaspoons) active dry yeast

1 cup sourdough starter

1 teaspoon kosher salt

5 ½ to 6 cups bread or all-purpose flour, divided

½ cup (1 stick) unsalted butter, softened

Lodge brand cast iron bread pans are great for making bread. Place a pan of water on the rack below the bread in the oven. The steam created will make a crunchy crust.

SOURDOUGH STARTER Combine the dry yeast with the water. Whisk in the sugar, flour, and salt. Let sit uncovered on the counter for 4–6 days. Whisk 4–5 times daily.

BREAD Scald the milk in a small saucepan. Stir in the sugar to dissolve. Let cool to lukewarm. Pour the warm water into the bowl of a standing mixer or a large bowl; sprinkle with yeast and stir until dissolved. Add the milk mixture, sourdough starter, salt, and 3 cups of the flour. Mix with the dough hook until smooth. Cut the butter into pieces and incorporate. Add enough of the remaining flour to make a smooth dough.

Turn dough out onto a floured surface and knead until smooth and elastic, 4-5 minutes. Form into a ball and place into a greased bowl, turning to coat all sides. Cover with plastic wrap and let rise in a warm place until doubled, 1–1 ¼ hours.

Punch dough down and let rest for about 15 minutes. Grease two 9 x 5-inch loaf pans. Divide the dough in half and shape into loaves. Transfer the dough to the loaf pans and make a cut on the top of each loaf with a sharp knife. Spray some plastic wrap with cooking spray, so that it doesn't stick, and loosely cover the loaves. Let rise until doubled, 1–1 ¼ hours.

Preheat the oven to 400 degrees F. Bake for about 40 minutes, or until golden brown. Let cool for 10 minutes. Remove from bread pans and let cool completely.

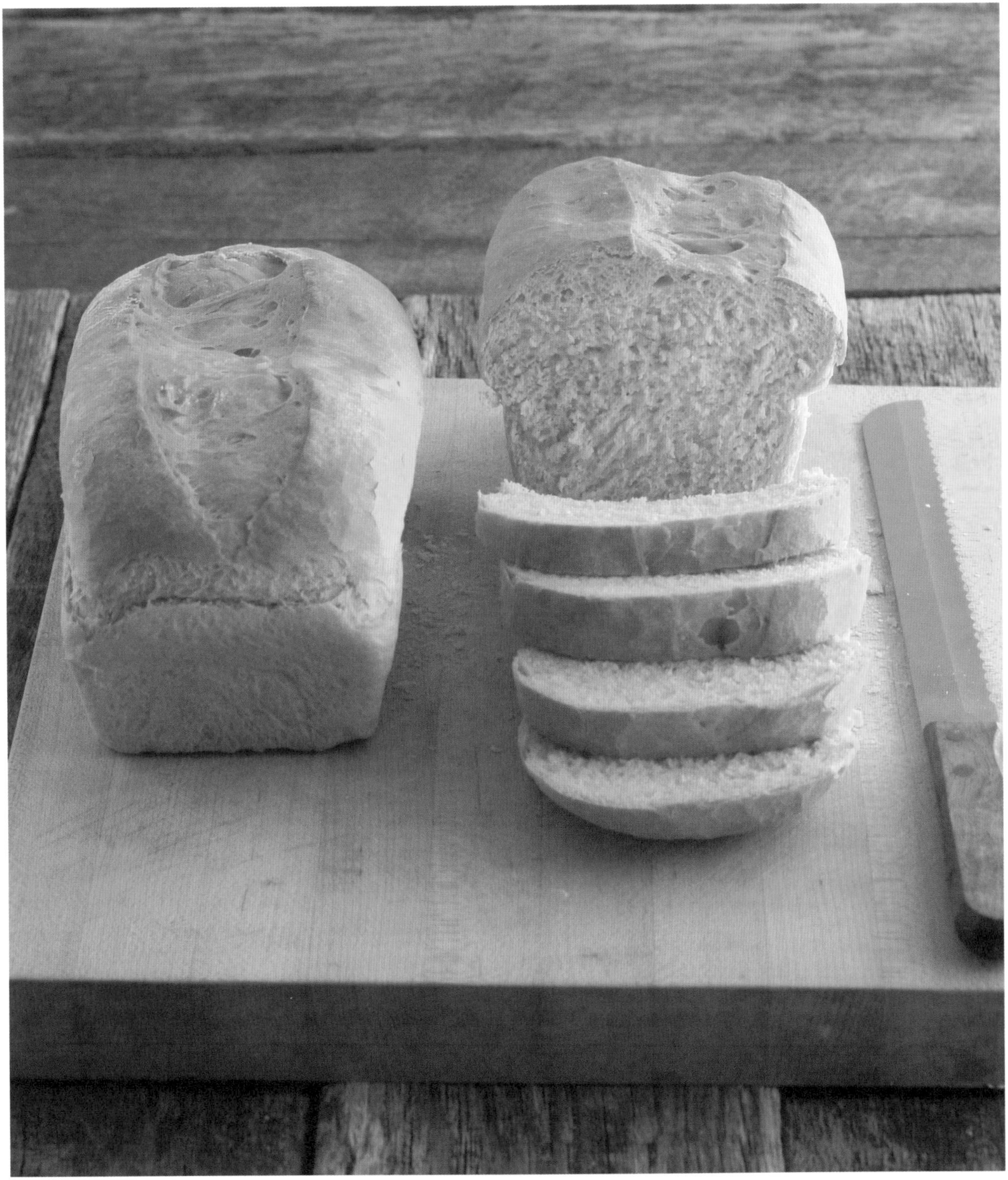

LEMON POUND CAKE

MAKES 2 LOAVES

The scent of lemon will fill your kitchen as this cake bakes. This is one of my favorite cakes from my childhood, and customers always love it at the farmers market.

CAKE

- 1 3/4 cups granulated sugar
- 1 cup (2 sticks) unsalted butter, softened
- 4 large eggs, room temperature
- 3/4 cup full-fat sour cream
- 2 teaspoons pure lemon oil
- 1/4 cup freshly squeezed lemon juice
- 3 cups all-purpose or cake flour
- 1 teaspoon baking powder
- 1/2 teaspoon baking soda
- 1 teaspoon kosher salt

GLAZE

- 1 1/2 cups powdered sugar
- 2 tablespoons freshly squeezed lemon juice
- 1 to 2 tablespoons whole milk

CAKE Cream together the sugar and butter in the bowl of a stand mixer, or in a large bowl using an electric hand mixer. Add the eggs, one at a time, and incorporate. Add the sour cream, lemon oil, and lemon juice. Sift together the flour, baking powder, baking soda, and salt. Add the sifted flour mixture to the sour cream mixture and incorporate just until smooth. Scrape the bottom and the sides of the bowl occasionally with a rubber spatula.

Preheat the oven to 350 degrees F. Spray two 9 x 5-inch loaf pans with cooking spray. Pour the cake batter evenly into the pans. Smooth the batter with a rubber spatula. Bake for 55–60 minutes, until a toothpick inserted into the center comes out clean. Let cool for 15–20 minutes before drizzling with glaze.

GLAZE Simply whisk together all the ingredients until smooth.

PEANUT BUTTER–COCONUT GRANOLA BARS

» MAKES 15 TO 18 BARS

This is one of my favorite go-to granola bars for heading out to horse shows for the weekend. It gives me a burst of energy with touches of peanut butter, maple syrup, and shredded coconut.

4 cups old-fashioned rolled oats
2 cups all-purpose flour
1 teaspoon kosher salt
1 teaspoon baking powder
½ cup firmly packed brown sugar
¾ cup creamy peanut butter
½ cup sweetened shredded coconut
¾ cup semisweet chocolate chips
½ cup chopped pecans
½ cup pure maple syrup or honey
½ cup (1 stick) butter, softened, or vegetable oil
1 teaspoon pure vanilla extract

Preheat the oven to 350 degrees F. Line a 9 x 13-inch pan with parchment paper and lightly grease with cooking spray.

In a large bowl, combine the oats, flour, salt, baking powder, brown sugar, and peanut butter. Add the coconut, chocolate chips, pecans, maple syrup, butter, and vanilla until the mixture is evenly crumbly. Spread in the prepared pan and gently pat down the mixture until flat.

Bake the bars for 25–30 minutes, until lightly golden brown. Remove pan from the oven, set on a cooling rack, and let cool for about 5 minutes. Use a sharp knife or bench knife to cut the bars. Cool completely before storing in an airtight container or wrapping individually with plastic wrap. During humid weather, store in the refrigerator. The bars can be stored for up to 1 week.

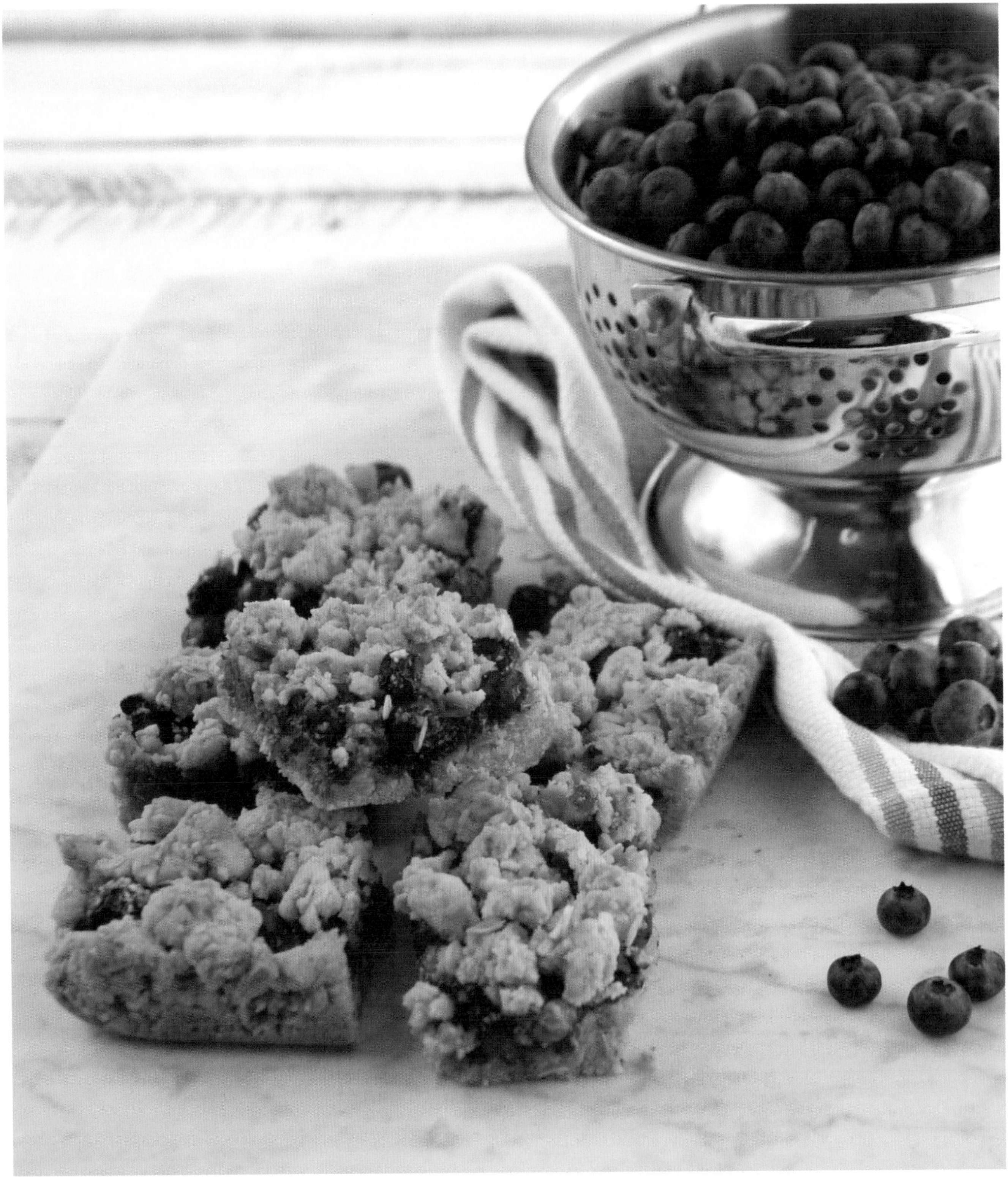

BLUEBERRY CRUMBLE BARS

» MAKES 15 TO 18 BARS

This delicious dessert reminds me of many summers we spent in Maine and all of the roadside stands selling wild blueberries. I love their simplicity.

1 cup (2 sticks) unsalted butter
1 cup firmly packed brown sugar
1 cup granulated sugar
1 large egg, room temperature
2 teaspoons pure vanilla extract
3 cups all-purpose flour
2 cups old-fashioned rolled oats
1 teaspoon kosher salt
1 teaspoon baking powder
3 cups fresh or frozen blueberries
3 tablespoons freshly squeezed lemon juice
1/4 cup granulated sugar
3 tablespoons instant tapioca

Preheat the oven to 350 degrees F. Spray a 9 x 13-inch baking dish with cooking spray, or brush with butter.

In the bowl of a stand mixer, or in a large bowl using an electric hand mixer, cream together the butter, brown sugar, and granulated sugar. Add the egg and vanilla and combine. Stir in the flour, oats, salt, and baking powder until incorporated. In a medium bowl, stir together the blueberries, lemon juice, sugar, and tapioca and set aside.

Press half of the crumble mixture into the bottom of the prepared pan. Spread the blueberry mixture evenly over the crust. Gently crumble the remaining crust mixture over the blueberries. Bake for 45–50 minutes, until lightly golden brown. Cool completely before cutting into bars.

BLUEBERRY CAKE DOUGHNUTS

»» MAKES 18 DOUGHNUTS AND HOLES

This doughnut recipe is easy to make and very delicious. Make them the night before and fry them fresh in the morning.

DOUGHNUTS

3 ½ cups all-purpose or cake flour
1 teaspoon kosher salt
1 tablespoon baking powder
6 tablespoons unsalted butter, softened
⅔ cup granulated sugar
2 teaspoons pure vanilla extract
2 large eggs, room temperature
1 cup full-fat sour cream
1 cup wild blueberries
Canola oil, for frying

GLAZE

2 cups powdered sugar
½ teaspoon pure vanilla extract
2 tablespoons whole milk

DOUGHNUTS Sift together the flour, salt, and baking powder into a medium bowl and set aside. In the bowl of a stand mixer, or in a large bowl using an electric hand mixer, cream together the butter and sugar until smooth. Add the vanilla and eggs and combine. Add the sour cream and combine. Gently incorporate the flour mixture until well combined. Scrape the bottom and sides of the bowl occasionally with a rubber spatula. Gently fold in the blueberries.

Line a baking sheet with parchment paper and set aside. Turn the dough out onto a well-floured work surface and use a rolling pin to roll out the dough to ½-inch thickness. Lightly flour a doughnut cutter, cut out the doughnuts, and place them onto the prepared baking sheet.

Line another baking sheet with several layers of paper towels and set aside. In a large heavy-duty pot, heat about 3 inches of canola oil to 375 degrees F. Drop about 4 doughnuts into the oil, making sure not to overcrowd the pot. Cook for 1–2 minutes on each side, until lightly golden brown. Remove the doughnuts from the oil and allow to drain on the paper towels.

GLAZE Combine all the ingredients in a small bowl and whisk until smooth. Line a baking sheet with parchment paper and set a cooling rack on top of the paper. Dip each doughnut into the glaze and let drip-dry on the rack.

MARKET PANTRY
UNSALTED
BUTTER
made with SWEET CREAM
STICKS 4

PASTRY WITH BERRIES

» SERVES 6 TO 8

This is one of my favorite desserts to make with fresh berries from the farmers market. The pastry cream is inspired by my grandmother's recipe. You'll be licking every last drop out of the bowl.

SHORTBREAD PASTRY CRUST

¾ cup (1 ½ sticks) unsalted butter, softened

½ cup powdered sugar

2 cups all-purpose flour

½ teaspoon kosher salt

3 tablespoons buttermilk, cold

½ teaspoon almond extract

FILLING

1 (3.4-ounce) package instant lemon or vanilla pudding

2 cups whole milk

1 teaspoon almond extract

1 pint heavy whipping cream

Fresh berries (such as strawberries, raspberries, or blueberries), for topping

SHORTBREAD PASTRY CRUST Cream together the butter and sugar in the bowl of a stand mixer, or in a large bowl using an electric hand mixer. Sift together the flour and salt and mix into the creamed butter mixture. Add the buttermilk and almond extract and mix until combined. Form the dough into a flat round and transfer to a ziplock bag or wrap with plastic wrap. Refrigerate for 1–2 hours.

FILLING Whisk the pudding, milk, and almond extract until smooth in a large bowl. Cover with plastic wrap and refrigerate for 1–2 hours. Using an electric hand mixer, beat the heavy whipping cream in a medium bowl until stiff peaks form. Cover and set in the refrigerator.

Preheat the oven to 350 degrees F. Remove the dough from the refrigerator. Using your fingers, press the dough evenly into a 12-inch tart pan with a removable bottom. Press the dough gently into the indentations in the sides of the pan. Use a fork to poke a few holes in the bottom of the crust so air can escape. Bake for 20–25 minutes, until lightly golden brown. Let cool completely.

To finish, gently fold the whipped cream and the pudding mixture together. Fill the crust then top with berries. Refrigerate until ready to serve.

LEMON-GINGER SCONES

» MAKES 10 TO 12 SCONES

Two bright flavors have been combined into a flaky and buttery scone. Scones can be made ahead of time and baked directly from the freezer.

2 ¾ cups all-purpose flour, plus more for sprinkling

¼ cup granulated sugar

1 teaspoon kosher salt

1 tablespoon baking powder

½ cup (1 stick) unsalted butter, very cold

2 large eggs

2 teaspoons pure lemon oil

⅔ cup buttermilk, cold

½ cup candied ginger chips

Heavy whipping cream, for coating

Sugar crystals, for sprinkling

In a large bowl, whisk together the flour, sugar, salt, and baking powder. Put the bowl into the freezer to chill. In the bowl of a stand mixer, or in a large bowl using an electric hand mixer, combine the chilled flour mixture with the butter just until crumbly. In a separate measuring cup or bowl, whisk together the eggs, lemon oil, and buttermilk. Add the buttermilk mixture to the flour mixture and stir until everything is moistened and holds together. Gently fold in the ginger chips.

Transfer the dough to a parchment-lined sheet pan. Sprinkle with a little flour and flatten down with your hands. Cover with plastic wrap and refrigerate for 4–6 hours. Turn the dough out onto a lightly floured surface and roll out into a rectangle shape about ¾ inch thick. Cut diagonally to make triangles. Place the scones onto a parchment-lined sheet pan, leaving a little bit of space between each one. Cover with plastic wrap and place the scones in the freezer for 1–2 hours.

Preheat the oven to 425 degrees F. Remove the scones from the freezer, brush with the cream, and sprinkle with sugar crystals. Bake for 20–25 minutes, until golden brown. The scones should not be soft when you press on the centers. Transfer the scones to a cooling rack for 5–10 minutes. Enjoy warm, or let cool completely before putting into a plastic bag for storage.

LEMON-BLUEBERRY SCONES

» MAKES 10 TO 12 SCONES

I created this scone recipe a few years back using local blueberries and lemon Greek yogurt from a Connecticut dairy farm. It's one of my favorite additions to a weekend breakfast or brunch. Scones can be made ahead of time and baked directly from the freezer.

- 2 3/4 cups all-purpose flour, plus more for sprinkling
- 1/4 cup granulated sugar
- 1 teaspoon kosher salt
- 1 tablespoon baking powder
- 1/2 cup (1 stick) unsalted butter, very cold
- 2 large eggs
- 2 teaspoons pure lemon oil
- 3/4 cup lemon Greek yogurt
- 1 cup fresh blueberries
- Heavy whipping cream, for coating
- Sugar crystals, for sprinkling

In a large bowl, whisk together the flour, sugar, salt, and baking powder. Put the bowl into the freezer to chill. In the bowl of a stand mixer, or in a large bowl using an electric hand mixer, combine the chilled flour mixture with the butter just until crumbly. In a separate measuring cup or bowl, whisk together the eggs, lemon oil, and Greek yogurt. Add the yogurt mixture to the flour mixture and stir until everything is moistened and holds together. Gently fold in the blueberries.

Transfer the dough to a parchment-lined sheet pan. Sprinkle with a little flour and flatten down with your hands. Cover with plastic wrap and refrigerate for 4–6 hours. Turn the dough out onto a lightly floured surface and roll out into a rectangle shape about 3/4 inch thick. Cut diagonally to make triangles. Place the scones onto a parchment-lined sheet pan, leaving a little bit of space between each one. Cover with plastic wrap and place the scones in the freezer for 1–2 hours.

Preheat the oven to 425 degrees F. Remove the scones from the freezer, brush with the cream, and sprinkle with sugar crystals. Bake for 20–25 minutes, until golden brown. The scones should not be soft when you press on the centers. Transfer the scones to a cooling rack for 5–10 minutes. Enjoy warm, or let cool completely before putting into a plastic bag for storage.

COCONUT-PINEAPPLE CAKE

»» MAKES 2 (8-INCH) ROUND CAKES

Layered with pineapple custard filling and covered in coconut flakes, this fluffy cake is a Southern tradition.

CAKE

- 4 large eggs, room temperature, separated
- ½ teaspoon cream of tartar
- 1 cup (2 sticks) unsalted butter, softened
- 2 cups granulated sugar
- 1 teaspoon pure vanilla extract
- 1 teaspoon coconut extract
- 1 cup full-fat sour cream
- ½ cup whole milk
- 3 cups all-purpose or cake flour
- 1 tablespoon baking powder
- 1 teaspoon kosher salt

PINEAPPLE CUSTARD

- ½ cup granulated sugar
- 2 tablespoons unsalted butter
- ¼ cup cornstarch
- 1 (20-ounce) can crushed pineapple
- 1 teaspoon pure vanilla extract

FROSTING

- 1 pound powdered sugar
- 1 cup vegetable shortening
- ¼ cup evaporated milk, lukewarm, plus more as needed
- ½ teaspoon kosher salt
- 1 cup sweetened flaked coconut

Preheat the oven to 350 degrees F. Spray two 8-inch round pans with cooking spray, sprinkle with flour, and tap out excess flour. Set aside.

CAKE Beat the egg whites and cream of tartar in a clean, dry ceramic bowl, using an electric hand mixer, until stiff peaks form. Set aside. In the bowl of a stand mixer, or in a large bowl using an electric hand mixer, cream together the butter, sugar, vanilla, and coconut extract. Add the egg yolks, one at a time, combining well. Add the sour cream, milk, flour, baking powder, and salt; mix for 2–3 minutes. Using a rubber spatula, gently fold in the egg whites. Make sure the batter is thoroughly combined. Scoop the batter into the prepared pans. Bake for 20–25 minutes, until a toothpick inserted into the center comes out clean. Let cakes cool for 5–10 minutes before transferring the cakes from the pans to a cooling rack. Let cool completely. While the cakes cool, make the custard.

PINEAPPLE CUSTARD Combine the sugar, butter, cornstarch, and pineapple with juice in a medium saucepan. Cook over medium heat, stirring constantly with a wooden spoon so it does not burn. Cook until mixture is bubbling and starts to thicken, 4–5 minutes. Remove from heat and add the vanilla. Let cool completely.

FROSTING Gently beat together the powdered sugar, shortening, evaporated milk, and salt in the bowl of a stand mixer, or in a large bowl using an electric hand mixer. Increase the speed to high and whip the frosting until fluffy. Add more evaporated milk if necessary.

To finish, transfer 1 cake to a plate or a cardboard round covered in aluminum foil. Spread the pineapple custard evenly across the center of the cake, leaving 1–2 inches around the edge. Place the second layer of cake on top. Frost sides and top of cake, sprinkle with coconut, and press remaining coconut into the sides.

OLD-FASHIONED SUGAR COOKIES

» MAKES 48 COOKIES

These delicious cookies are full of simple, old-fashioned goodness. Roll them in different colored sugars, chopped nuts, or crushed candy canes for festiveness. This versatile cookie dough can be made into jam thumbprint cookies as well.

3 cups granulated sugar

1 ½ cups (3 sticks) unsalted butter, softened

1 teaspoon pure vanilla extract

½ teaspoon almond extract

4 large eggs, room temperature

5 ½ cups all-purpose flour

1 teaspoon kosher salt

1 teaspoon baking powder

Colored sugars, for decorating

In the bowl of a stand mixer, or in a large bowl using an electric hand mixer, cream together the sugar and butter. Add the vanilla, almond extract, and eggs, one at a time. Occasionally scrape the bottom and sides of the bowl with a rubber spatula. In another bowl, sift together the flour, salt, and baking powder. Incorporate the flour mixture into the sugar mixture until combined.

Preheat the oven to 350 degrees F.

Roll dough into 2-inch rounds and roll into various colored sugars. Transfer cookies to parchment-lined sheet pans, leaving space in between for them to spread a little. Bake for about 15 minutes, until lightly golden brown. Transfer cookies to a cooling rack.

FARMGIRL HOMESTEADING
COOKING FROM SCRATCH

HANDCRAFTED FOOD BRINGS SO MUCH JOY TO ME, AND THAT FEELING GREW OUT OF MY CHILDHOOD FARMING LIFE. Some people may see my brother and me as having been deprived, with no fancy food, toys, or store-bought dolls. But my mom poured her talent and love into everything she made, creating things more special than any advertised on television.

My mom made wedding cakes for nearly thirty years, and those creations were stunning. She spent hours in the sugarhouse handcrafting gum paste and sugar flowers to decorate the cakes. Each handmade sugar flower was dried thoroughly in a dehydrator before she carefully dusted each individual petal with a touch of color. After they had dried, the flowers were packed in a plastic container, layered with parchment or wax paper to prevent possible damage, and sealed with a lid.

Unfortunately, my mom suffered from severe migraines. She would spend several days in bed sick—dishes piled up, laundry and housekeeping fell behind. If a migraine came on when she needed to complete a cake, my brother and I would step in to help assemble the elaborate creation. In turn, both of us received hands-on cake decorating lessons. We also learned lessons in turning around disasters.

One humid, hot summer day, I helped my mom carry a cake on an hour-long back road journey to its destination. The cake started melting in the car, making the icing run and fall. My mom worked her magic to make the five-tier cake look even more like the magazine clipping the bride had asked her to recreate than when she started. I learned not only that every potential failure can be turned into a success, but also that food created by loving, talented hands, whether it's for a backyard barbeque or a special occasion, will always outshine anything from a box or a jar and create memories that last for generations.

BROWN SUGAR–MUSTARD CHICKEN

»» SERVES 6

The sweet and spicy marinated chicken breasts remain moist while grilling and brown sugar caramelizes. This chicken is incredible as a sandwich or sliced on top of a fresh garden salad. Try Mustard Girl Zesty Horseradish in this marinade for an extra zing of flavor.

- 4 to 5 pounds boneless, skinless chicken breasts
- ⅓ cup firmly packed brown sugar
- ¼ cup olive oil
- ⅓ cup stone-ground mustard
- 3 tablespoons balsamic vinegar
- 1 tablespoon onion powder
- 1 teaspoon garlic powder
- Salt and freshly ground black pepper, to taste

In a large ziplock bag or in between two layers of plastic wrap, use a meat tenderizer or a wooden rolling pin to pound the chicken to about ¾-inch thickness.

In another large ziplock bag, combine the brown sugar, olive oil, mustard, balsamic vinegar, onion powder, garlic powder, salt, and pepper. Swirl the ingredients around with your fingers from the outside of the bag. Place the flattened chicken breasts into the bag with the marinade. Marinate in the refrigerator for 2–6 hours or overnight.

Heat the grill to medium high, or heat 2 tablespoons olive oil and 1 tablespoon butter in a large skillet over medium high. Cook the chicken for about 3 minutes on each side. Let rest for a few minutes before slicing.

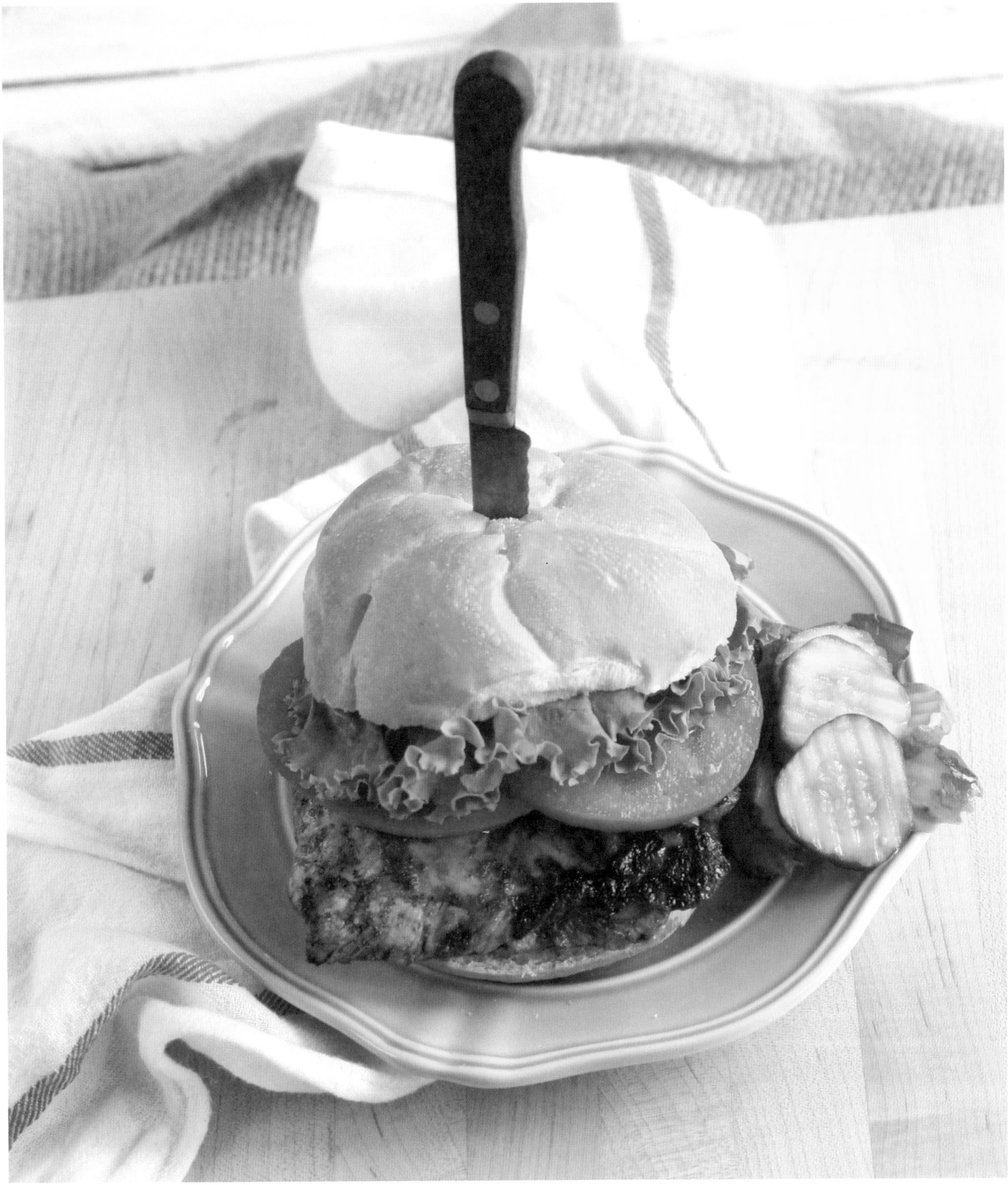

FARMHOUSE MEATBALLS

MAKES 24 TO 30 MEATBALLS

The smell of homemade meatballs cooking in the sugarhouse kitchen made me anticipate Sunday dinner. They're great on pasta, but I also like them paired with marinara sauce and melted cheese on a crusty roll. Cook a bunch and freeze them for quick dinners later.

- 3 pounds ground chuck (80–90 percent lean)
- 1 ½ cups grated Parmesan cheese
- 1 cup seasoned bread crumbs
- ¼ cup diced yellow onion
- ¼ cup fresh basil, chopped
- ¼ cup fresh parsley, chopped
- 2 teaspoons onion powder
- 1 teaspoon garlic powder
- 6 large eggs
- Salt and freshly ground black pepper, to taste
- 2 to 3 tablespoons olive oil
- Farmhouse Marinara Sauce, for serving (page 143)

In a large bowl, mix together the chuck, Parmesan, bread crumbs, onion, basil, parsley, onion powder, garlic powder, eggs, salt, and pepper. Shape mixture into 3-inch rounds and place on a plate. Heat the olive oil in a large pan over medium heat. Cook the meatballs in batches until browned on all sides and cooked all the way through, 20–25 minutes, using tongs to occasionally turn.

Serve with Farmhouse Marinara Sauce over spaghetti, or place on rolls, cover with the sauce, sprinkle with grated mozzarella cheese, and bake in the oven for meatball sandwiches.

FARMHOUSE MARINARA SAUCE

» MAKES ABOUT 7 (16-OUNCE) JARS

Alone or with Farmhouse Meatballs (page 142), this versatile sauce is a great basic recipe for any home cook. Make a big batch, can or freeze it, and you can quickly put a homemade meal on the table on a busy night.

½ cup extra virgin olive oil
2 large onions, chopped
10 cloves garlic, minced
6 cups water
12 cups tomato purée
3 (12-ounce) cans tomato paste
3 cups firmly packed brown sugar
2 tablespoons dried oregano
2 tablespoons dried fennel
1 tablespoon dried basil
1 tablespoon kosher salt
2 teaspoons freshly ground black pepper

In a 10 to 12-quart pot, heat the olive oil and cook the onions and garlic until the onions are softened but not browned. Once the onions are soft, add the water, tomato purée, tomato paste, brown sugar, oregano, fennel, basil, salt, and pepper. Use a metal whisk to remove any lumps. Adjust the salt and pepper as desired. Simmer over low heat until desired thickness is reached, stirring to keep it from scorching.

Scoop sauce into plastic deli containers, let cool, and then place in the freezer. Or ladle into glass jars, wipe rims clean with a damp paper towel, place lids on fingertip tight, and process in a water bath for 15 minutes (adjusting for altitude) to make shelf stable.

SOUTHERN BISCUITS AND SAUSAGE GRAVY

»» SERVES 5 TO 6

This recipe blends a traditional Southern-style breakfast with a twist from my New England roots. Be sure you offer plenty of homemade biscuits to sop up the gravy.

BISCUITS

2 ¾ cups all-purpose flour
1 tablespoon baking powder
½ teaspoon baking soda
1 teaspoon kosher salt
⅓ cup lard
4 tablespoons unsalted butter, cold
1 cup buttermilk, cold

SAUSAGE GRAVY

1 pound ground sweet sausage
1 tablespoon granulated maple sugar
4 tablespoons unsalted butter
¼ cup all-purpose flour
3 cups whole milk
Salt and freshly ground black pepper, to taste

Preheat the oven to 450 degrees F. Line a baking sheet with parchment paper and set aside.

BISCUITS Combine the flour, baking powder, baking soda, and salt in a large bowl. Use a fork or pastry cutter to cut the lard and butter into the flour until the mixture resembles coarse meal. Gradually stir in the buttermilk until the dough pulls away from the sides of the bowl.

Turn the dough out onto a lightly floured work surface. Gently knead the dough 10 to 15 times. Using a rolling pin, roll out the dough to about ½- to ¾-inch thickness. Use a biscuit cutter, 2 ½ to 3 inches in size, to cut out the biscuits from the dough. Place them on the prepared baking sheet. Bake until lightly golden brown, 15–16 minutes.

GRAVY Place the sausage in a large, deep skillet. Sprinkle with maple sugar. Cook over medium to high heat until browned. Use a slotted spoon to transfer the sausage to a separate dish, leaving the drippings in the pan. Stir in the butter until melted. Add the flour and stir until smooth. Reduce heat to medium and cook until light brown. Gradually whisk in the milk and cook until thickened. Add the cooked sausage back to the skillet. Season the gravy with salt and pepper. Reduce heat and simmer for 12–15 minutes, stirring frequently. If gravy becomes too thick, stir in a little more milk.

Serve the biscuits halved and smothered with gravy.

FARMHOUSE CHICKEN CASSEROLE

SERVES 6 TO 8

This is one of my favorite dishes to cook in the fall and winter. You can even add a head of cabbage cut into quarters.

- 8 slices bacon, chopped
- 2 tablespoons olive oil
- 4 to 5 pounds bone-in, skin-on chicken thighs
- 2 large onions, sliced
- 6 to 8 carrots, peeled and sliced
- 1/4 cup all-purpose flour
- 2 cups dry white wine (such as Pinot Grigio or Sauvignon Blanc)
- 2 cups chicken stock
- 2 teaspoons onion powder
- 1 teaspoon garlic powder
- Salt and freshly ground black pepper, to taste
- 18 to 20 pearl onions, peeled
- 1 pint baby portobella mushrooms, sliced
- 2 tablespoons butter
- 2 teaspoons dried parsley
- Roasted Garlic Mashed Potatoes (page 102), for serving

In a 6-quart enameled cast iron Dutch oven, sauté the bacon in the olive oil over medium heat. Once lightly browned, use a slotted spoon to transfer the bacon to a separate dish.

Sauté a few pieces of chicken at a time in the hot oil and bacon fat until they are evenly browned. Remove the chicken pieces and set aside. Brown the onions and carrots in the fat. Drain the cooking fat.

Preheat the oven to 325 degrees F. Over medium to high heat, sprinkle the carrots and onions with flour and stir with a wooden spoon to evenly coat. Cook for about 5 minutes to lightly brown the flour. Stir in the wine and chicken stock. Return the chicken and bacon to the pot and season with onion powder, garlic powder, salt, and pepper. Bring to a simmer, cover, and place in the middle of the oven for about 2 hours, until the chicken is fully cooked.

While the casserole is cooking, prepare the pearl onions and portobella mushrooms. Melt the butter in a large skillet over medium heat. Add the mushrooms and pearl onions and sauté for 10–15 minutes, until slightly soft. Pour the onions and mushrooms over the top of the casserole, sprinkle with the parsley, and serve over mashed potatoes.

STRAWBERRY SHORTCAKE

» MAKES 6 SHORTCAKES

Strawberries and rustic shortcakes are a simple, classic combination. We picked strawberries together as a family at another local farm, and it's quite a fond memory.

STRAWBERRIES

4 cups whole fresh strawberries, halved or quartered

¼ to ½ cup granulated sugar

WHIPPED CREAM

1 pint heavy whipping cream

2 tablespoons granulated sugar

SHORTCAKES

2 ½ cups all-purpose flour

¼ cup granulated sugar

1 teaspoon baking soda

2 teaspoons baking powder

1 teaspoon kosher salt

6 tablespoons unsalted butter, melted

1 cup buttermilk

STRAWBERRIES Mix the berries with the sugar in a medium bowl, cover with plastic wrap, and refrigerate until ready to serve. This will help draw out the natural juices in the strawberries.

WHIPPED CREAM Pour the cream and sugar into a large bowl. Use an electric hand mixer on high speed to beat until stiff peaks form. Cover with plastic wrap and place in the refrigerator.

SHORTCAKES Preheat the oven to 425 degrees F. Line a baking sheet with parchment paper. In a medium bowl, stir together the flour, sugar, baking soda, baking powder, salt, butter, and buttermilk until a soft dough forms. Drop dough by the spoonful onto the baking sheet. Bake for 12–14 minutes, until golden brown.

To finish, split the shortcakes with a knife and place in shallow bowls. Fill with strawberries and whipped cream.

GORGONZOLA-BACON STUFFED MUSHROOMS

» SERVES 6 TO 8

Serve these mushrooms as an appetizer or pair them with a char-grilled steak.

- ½ pound sweet sausage
- 20 to 24 baby portobella mushrooms
- 4 ounces cream cheese, room temperature
- 1 large egg, room temperature
- ½ cup unseasoned bread crumbs
- 6 slices bacon, cooked and chopped
- 1 teaspoon onion powder
- ½ teaspoon garlic powder
- Salt and freshly ground black pepper, to taste
- ⅔ cup crumbled Gorgonzola cheese

In a medium skillet over medium heat, brown the sausage. Set aside.

Line a 9 x 13-inch baking pan with parchment paper. Remove the mushroom stems from the caps. Place mushroom caps in the baking pan and chop the stems.

Preheat the oven to 350 degrees F. In a medium bowl, combine the cream cheese with the egg. Incorporate bread crumbs, bacon, mushroom stems, sausage, onion powder, garlic powder, salt, pepper, and Gorgonzola. Fill each mushroom cap generously with the sausage mixture. Bake for 45 minutes, or until the filling is a toasted golden brown.

PEANUT BUTTER CHOCOLATE CUPS

» MAKES 36 CANDIES

Who doesn't love chocolate and peanut butter? No baking is needed for this treat that combines two classic flavors, and they make a wonderful addition to your holiday cookie trays.

- 1 ½ cups powdered sugar
- 1 ½ cups creamy peanut butter
- ⅔ cup graham cracker crumbs
- 3 tablespoons unsalted butter, softened
- 3 cups semisweet chocolate chips

In the bowl of a stand mixer, or in a large bowl using an electric hand mixer, cream together the powdered sugar, peanut butter, graham cracker crumbs, and butter. Transfer to a plastic bag or pastry bag and set aside.

Melt the chocolate in a bowl set over simmering water. Keep melted chocolate over hot water near your work area. Line a half sheet pan with parchment paper. Place 36 mini cupcake papers on the sheet pan. Use a teaspoon to drizzle a little melted chocolate into the bottom of each paper. Transfer to the refrigerator for about 15 minutes to set.

Remove the chilled cups from the refrigerator, and pipe the peanut butter mixture evenly into the cups. Spoon melted chocolate over each cup to cover. Use the back of the spoon to spread the chocolate evenly over the peanut butter. Return to the refrigerator for 2 hours, or until set.

STRAWBERRY LEMONADE

»» SERVES 6 TO 8

I love making this sweet-tart strawberry lemonade at home. It's so simple to make, and you can adjust the sugar to the level you prefer.

- 2 cups fresh or frozen strawberries, plus more for garnish
- 4 ¼ cups water, divided
- 2 ½ cups granulated sugar
- 2 cups freshly squeezed lemon juice
- Ice cubes, for serving

In a medium saucepan over medium heat, cook the strawberries in ¼ cup of water until soft. Press the strawberries through a sieve. Discard the seeds and pulp. Let the juices cool.

Meanwhile, bring the remaining 4 cups water and sugar to a boil to create simple syrup. Let cool. Pour into a pitcher. Add the lemon juice and strawberry purée. Add enough ice cubes to fill the pitcher and garnish with additional strawberries before serving.

BLUEBERRY AND NECTARINE COFFEE CAKE

›› SERVES 6 TO 8

This cake is straight from the Lamothe family collection of heirloom recipes, but I've updated it with blueberries and nectarines. Pure maple syrup for sweetening gives this amazing cake a unique flavor from my farm roots.

CAKE

- ½ cup (1 stick) unsalted butter, softened
- ¾ cup pure maple syrup
- 2 teaspoons pure vanilla extract
- 3 large eggs, room temperature
- 2 ½ cups all-purpose or cake flour
- ½ teaspoon kosher salt
- 2 teaspoons baking powder
- 2 nectarines, thinly sliced
- ½ cup fresh blueberries

STREUSEL TOPPING

- ¼ cup (½ stick) unsalted butter, softened
- ½ cup all-purpose flour
- ⅓ cup granulated sugar
- ½ teaspoon ground cinnamon

Preheat the oven to 350 degrees F. Grease a 9-inch round cake pan and set aside.

CAKE Beat together the butter and maple syrup in the bowl of a stand mixer, or in a large bowl using an electric hand mixer. Add the vanilla extract then the eggs, one at a time, and beat well. Sift together the flour, salt, and baking powder. Incorporate the flour mixture into the butter mixture until blended. Occasionally scrape the bottom and sides of the bowl while mixing. Spoon the cake batter into the prepared pan. Arrange the nectarines in a circular pattern on top of the cake batter. Sprinkle the blueberries evenly over the nectarines.

STREUSEL TOPPING Combine all of the ingredients in a small bowl until crumbly. Scatter the topping over the fruit. Bake for 40–45 minutes, until a toothpick inserted into the center comes out clean.

BOUNTIFUL AUTUMN HARVEST
FROM FARM TO TABLE

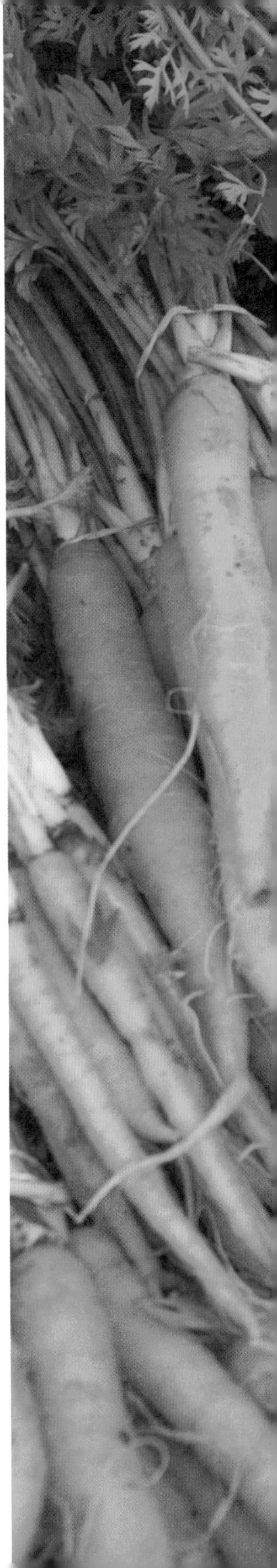

FROM THE FIRST COLD SNAP OF AUTUMN THROUGH THE WINTER HOLIDAYS, I THINK ABOUT HUMBLE, HEARTY FOOD FROM A SIMPLER TIME. As a farmer's daughter, my cooking and baking are not overly complicated and typically use ingredients you have in your pantry. I never attended formal culinary school. I'm an old-fashioned person who was brought up on recipes that were handed down through the generations. I learned much of what I know from my parents and was extremely fortunate to have a commercial kitchen at my disposal on the farm.

Grandma Lamothe told stories of growing up in a time when large families of six to ten children were not uncommon. Keeping a large vegetable garden to feed them all was part of everyday life, and kids helped with the associated chores. If you didn't grow it or make it yourself, you simply didn't have it. She recalled trading with other families or bartering with the butcher for necessities. Grandma said that growing up this particular way helped train young women to become wives, so transitioning into their running their own household went smoothly. There must be something right about the way my grandparents and parents were raised, because they are a generation of doers and go-getters.

Our parents were quite strict with us, and there was a reason behind it. Keeping tight reins on our every move kept us, for the most part, out of trouble. Frankly, they kept us so busy with chores on the farm, helping on other family farms, and schoolwork that we didn't have time to get into trouble. Today, we are raising our own children very much the same way—everyday chores, extremely limited technology, no cell phones, and making sure they have complete respect for others. Our oldest son, Camden, for example, is ring stewarding at horse shows throughout North Carolina nearly every weekend from spring to late fall. Some events are completely volunteer and others pay a small amount. That money gets saved to purchase essentials, new jeans, and anything he might need. It's teaching him how hard it is to earn a paycheck and how quickly it goes on things you need.

With a pitchfork, shovel, hoe, or garden hook in their hands, there's no time for a cell phone to be stuck into their faces. If the kids are going to eat this food too, why should you, as a parent, be putting in all the work? When the workday is over, the kids and everyone else will be ready to enjoy a meal from their labors. Here are a few tips that will keep the kitchen running smoothly:

- Always crack eggs into a separate bowl or glass measuring cup. Even with the freshest of laid eggs, you never know when you might get a bad one.
- Remove any hot mixture from the heat before adding vanilla extract (such as in caramel or peanut brittle), or the flavor will dissipate.
- A sealed bottle of maple syrup will last indefinitely. Once opened, you'll need to refrigerate it. If it does happen to get mold, pour into a small saucepan, bring to a boil and skim off the mold.
- Raw honey crystallizes, but it will never go bad. Liquefy it by placing the jar in a pan of simmering water for about 20 minutes. Do not refrigerate honey. (Note: It is not recommended to feed honey to a child under the age of one.)
- Every oven is different. For the most accurate temperature, use an oven-safe thermometer.
- Precut parchment paper half sheets fit your half sheet pans perfectly, making cleanup a breeze.

APPLE-CORNBREAD STUFFED PORK

» SERVES 10 TO 12

Let the Thanksgiving feast begin! This moist pork roast is perfect for any family gathering or Sunday dinner. Turkey is more traditional, but with our family farm raising hogs, we had an abundance of fresh pork.

1 tablespoon extra virgin olive oil

2 tablespoons butter

1 medium onion, finely chopped

3 stalks celery, finely chopped

2 large Granny Smith apples, peeled and chopped

1 large egg

4 tablespoons unsalted butter, softened

3 cups cornbread stuffing mix

1 cup dried cranberries

1 ½ cups apple cider, divided

2 teaspoons onion powder

1 teaspoon garlic powder

1 teaspoon dried sage or finely chopped fresh sage

¼ cup fresh parsley, finely chopped

Salt and freshly ground black pepper, to taste

1 (4- to 5-pound) boneless pork tenderloin

1 tablespoon cornstarch

1 cup water, warm

In a large skillet over medium heat, melt the olive oil and butter. Add the onion, celery, and apples and cook for 10 minutes, or until slightly translucent. Stir occasionally with a wooden spoon so they don't burn. Let cool.

Transfer the apple mixture to a large bowl and combine with the egg, softened butter, stuffing mix, cranberries, ½ cup of the apple cider, onion powder, garlic powder, sage, and parsley. Season with salt and pepper.

Butterfly the pork by making a deep incision down the length of the tenderloin to within ½ inch of the opposite side. Do not cut all the way through. Open the meat like a book so the tenderloin lies flat. Cover the pork with plastic wrap and pound with the flat side of a meat mallet to about ½ inch thick.

Preheat the oven to 450 degrees F.

Spread stuffing mixture over tenderloin. Starting with a long side, tightly roll up the tenderloin. Tie meat with butcher's twine to secure the shape. Season the tenderloin all over with salt and pepper. Place in a roasting pan. Pour the remaining 1 cup apple cider around the pork. Bake for 20 minutes then reduce oven temperature to 350 degrees F. Bake for an additional 45–60 minutes, until a thermometer reads 145 degrees F. Remove pork from pan, cover, and let stand for 10 minutes.

To make gravy, stir the cornstarch into the water until smooth. Pour cornstarch mixture into the roasting pan with the meat juices. Cook on the stovetop over medium to high heat, whisking as you go to remove any lumps. Serve with the pork or pour over the top.

CHEDDAR-CHIVE POPOVERS

MAKES 6 POPOVERS

Light and airy popovers are a traditional accompaniment for our Thanksgiving feast. They are also fabulous with homemade jam for breakfast or brunch.

- 4 large eggs, room temperature
- 1 ½ cups whole milk, lukewarm
- 1 tablespoon honey
- ½ teaspoon kosher salt
- 1 ½ cups all-purpose flour
- 4 tablespoons unsalted butter, melted
- ¼ cup grated cheddar cheese
- 2 tablespoons finely chopped chives

Preheat the oven to 425 degrees F. Position a rack closer to the bottom of the oven. Generously grease the popover pan with cooking spray, including the space between each cup.

In a medium bowl, use a wire whisk to beat the eggs, milk, honey, and salt until well combined. Add the flour and whisk vigorously until frothy. Stir in the butter. Fold in the cheese and chives with a rubber spatula. Scoop or pour the batter into the prepared pan, filling the cups three-quarters full. Place the pan in the oven and bake for about 20 minutes. Do not open the oven. After 20 minutes, lower the temperature to 350 degrees F and continue baking for 10–15 minutes, until golden brown. Serve immediately.

MAPLE-APPLE HONEY HAM

SERVES 8 TO 10

Ham is a holiday tradition, and we found ways to add maple flavor to just about everything at my house. This combination of maple syrup, cloves, pineapple, and apples makes this moist ham even more tasty.

- 1 (10- to 12-pound) spiral-cut ham
- 1 baking apple (such as Braeburn or McIntosh), peeled and cut into ½-inch-thick slices
- ¼ cup pure maple syrup
- 1 (12-ounce) can lemon-lime soda or ginger ale
- 8 fresh or canned pineapple slices
- 12 whole cloves

Preheat the oven to 300 degrees F.

Place ham into a roasting pan and stuff the apple slices in between the slices of ham. Drizzle with maple syrup and pour the can of soda over the ham. Place the pineapple slices on the top of the ham with the whole cloves. Cover the pan with aluminum foil and bake for 45–60 minutes. Occasionally spoon the pan juices over the ham to keep moist.

MAPLE APPLE BUTTER

»» MAKES 8 TO 10 (8-OUNCE) JARS

This old-fashioned treat has been handed down in my family for generations. We've added a touch of maple to give it a very unique flavor.

- 6 pounds baking apples (such as such as Macoun or Granny Smith), quartered
- 2 cups apple cider
- 1 tablespoon cornstarch
- 1/4 cup water, hot
- 1 cup firmly packed brown sugar
- 1 cup pure maple syrup
- 1 1/2 teaspoons ground cinnamon
- 1 teaspoon ground nutmeg
- 1/4 teaspoon ground cloves

In a large pot, cook the apples in the apple cider for 20–30 minutes, covered, until soft. Press cooked apples through a sieve or pass through a food mill. Discard skins and seeds.

Dissolve the cornstarch in the water. Add the dissolved cornstarch, brown sugar, maple syrup, cinnamon, nutmeg, and cloves to the apples. Whisk to incorporate everything well. Cook apple purée over medium heat, stirring occasionally with a wooden spoon. Be careful not to burn. Cook for 20–30 minutes, until desired thickness is reached.

Prepare a boiling water canner. Heat the jars and lids in simmering water until ready for use. Do not boil. Set bands aside.

Ladle hot apple butter into hot jars, leaving 1/2-inch headspace. Wipe the rims with a clean, damp paper towel. Center the lids on the jars. Apply the bands until the fit is fingertip tight. Process jars in the boiling water canner for 15 minutes, adjusting for altitude. Remove the jars and allow to cool. Check the lids for seal after 24 hours. The lid should not flex up and down when the center is pressed. Store jars in a cool, dry place. If a jar doesn't seal, store in the refrigerator for up to 8 weeks.

SPICED PUMPKIN BUTTER

» MAKES ABOUT 3 (16-OUNCE) JARS

This tastes like pumpkin pie in a jar. Spread it on toast, or swirl it into a cheesecake before baking for an unusual dessert for the Thanksgiving table or Sunday supper.

3 cups pumpkin purée

½ cup pure maple syrup

⅓ cup firmly packed brown sugar

1 ½ teaspoons freshly squeezed lemon juice

1 teaspoon ground cinnamon

½ teaspoon ground nutmeg

½ teaspoon ground ginger

⅛ teaspoon ground cloves

¼ teaspoon kosher salt

1 tablespoon cornstarch

¼ cup water, hot

Mix the pumpkin, maple syrup, brown sugar, lemon juice, cinnamon, nutmeg, ginger, cloves, and salt thoroughly in a large pot. Cook the mixture over medium heat until thick, stirring frequently with a wooden spoon. Dissolve the cornstarch in the water then stir into the pumpkin mixture. This will help it thicken. Be careful not to burn the mixture. Cool completely and store in an airtight container in the refrigerator for up to 2 weeks.

BRUNSWICK STEW

» SERVES 6 TO 8

Being new to North Carolina, I was asked by Bob Keen Sr., who owns the horse barn I ride at, if I had ever had Brunswick stew. I had not, so he brought me a big cup from a local barbeque joint and I fell in love. This recipe is created with that first taste in mind.

8 to 10 slices bacon, chopped

6 tablespoons butter

1 large onion, chopped

3 cloves garlic, minced

1 (15-ounce) can crushed tomatoes

4 cups chicken stock

1 tablespoon tomato paste

1 ½ cups prepared barbeque sauce

3 tablespoons Worcestershire sauce

¼ cup firmly packed brown sugar

1 ½ pounds pulled pork (Yankee Barbeque, page 54)

1 pound shredded chicken

3 large russet potatoes, peeled and cut into ½-inch cubes

3 cups corn kernels

2 cups fresh or frozen (thawed) baby lima beans

2 cups fresh or frozen (thawed) green beans

¼ teaspoon cayenne pepper

2 teaspoons onion powder

1 teaspoon garlic powder

Salt and freshly ground black pepper, to taste

Cook the bacon in a large Dutch oven over medium to high heat until crispy, 15–20 minutes. Line a plate with paper towels. Remove bacon from the pot with a slotted spoon and place on the paper towels. Set aside.

Add the butter to the pan to melt. Add the onion and garlic and sauté until soft, 3–4 minutes. Stir in the bacon, crushed tomatoes, stock, tomato paste, barbeque sauce, Worcestershire sauce, brown sugar, pork, chicken, potatoes, corn, lima beans, green beans, cayenne, onion powder, garlic powder, salt, and pepper. Bring the mixture to a boil, reduce to a simmer, and cook over low to medium heat until thick, about 1 hour. Stir occasionally with a wooden spoon to make sure nothing sticks or burns.

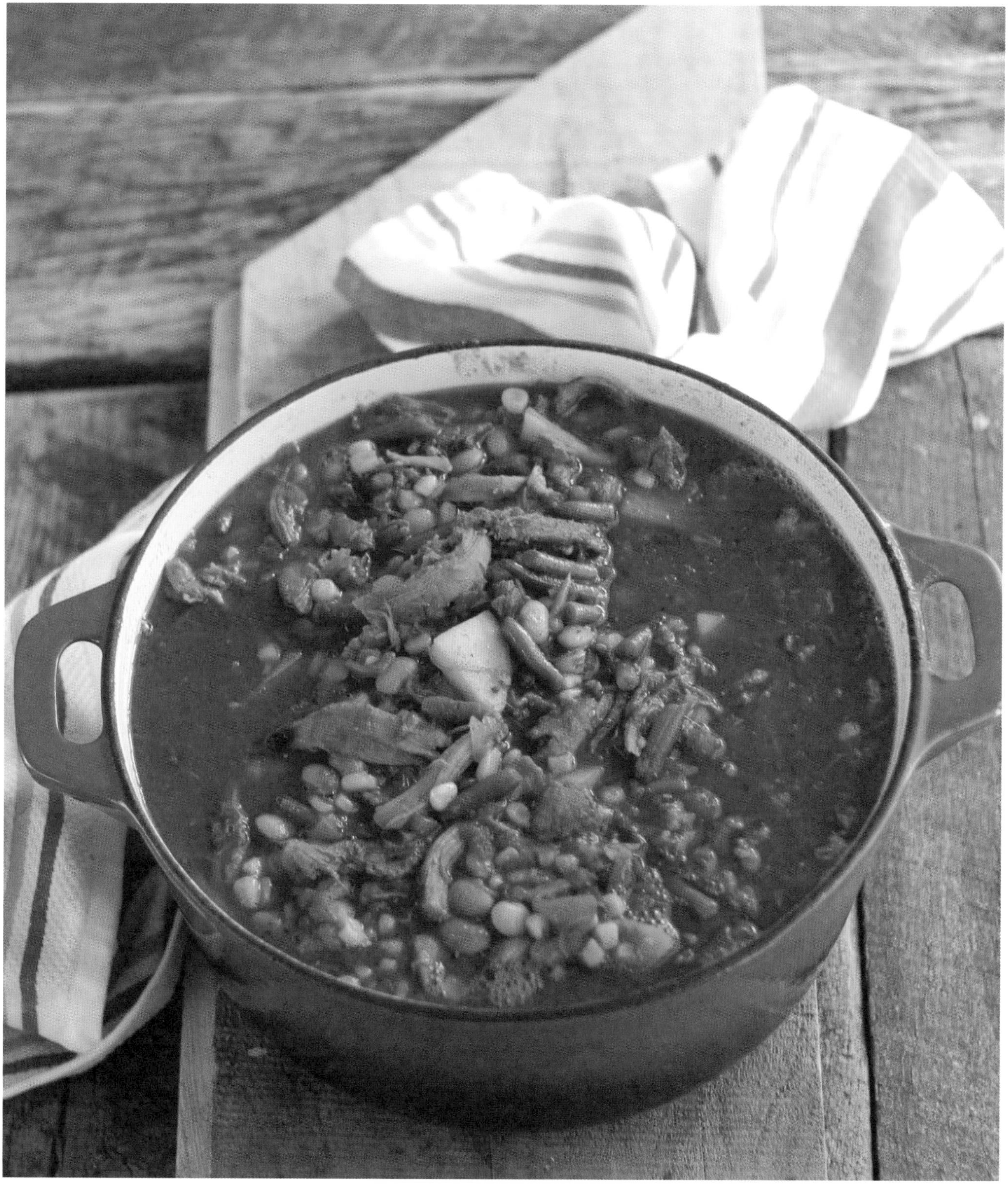

APPLE STREUSEL OAT MUFFINS

» MAKES 12 MUFFINS

These muffins are packed with rolled oats, wheat germ, apples, and cinnamon. Maple sugar is the dry form of maple syrup and can be substituted for equal parts in any recipe that calls for granulated sugar.

STREUSEL TOPPING

¼ cup (½ stick) unsalted butter, softened

½ cup wheat germ

½ cup old-fashioned rolled oats

½ cup chopped pecans

½ cup firmly packed brown sugar

½ cup all-purpose flour

MUFFINS

½ cup (1 stick) unsalted butter, softened

½ cup firmly packed brown sugar

½ cup granulated maple sugar

2 large eggs, room temperature

1 teaspoon pure vanilla extract

1 teaspoon kosher salt

1 cup full-fat sour cream

1 ½ cups all-purpose flour

½ cup old-fashioned rolled oats

¼ cup wheat germ

1 teaspoon baking powder

1 cup chopped baking apples (such as Macoun or Granny Smith)

STREUSEL TOPPING Add all the ingredients to a medium bowl. Mix with your hands until combined. Set aside.

Preheat the oven to 350 degrees F. Line a muffin pan with 12 paper liners and set aside.

MUFFINS Cream together the butter, brown sugar, and maple sugar in the bowl of a standing mixer, or in a large bowl using an electric hand mixer. Add the eggs, one at a time. Add the vanilla, salt, and sour cream and combine. Occasionally scrape the bottom and sides of the bowl with a rubber spatula. Add the flour, rolled oats, wheat germ, and baking powder and continue mixing until smooth. Fold in the apples.

Scoop the batter evenly into the paper liners, about three-fourths full. Sprinkle with the topping. Bake for about 30 minutes, until a toothpick inserted into the center comes out clean. Let cool slightly before removing muffins carefully from the pan.

PUMPKIN CHEESECAKE

» MAKES 1 (9-INCH) CHEESECAKE

Combining vanilla wafers with graham crackers makes an unusual crust for this cheesecake, which boasts the classic flavors of autumn.

CHEESECAKE

12 ounces cream cheese, softened
¾ cup granulated sugar
3 large eggs
1 cup full-fat sour cream
1 cup pumpkin purée
½ cup heavy whipping cream
1 teaspoon pure vanilla extract
1 teaspoon ground cinnamon
½ teaspoon ground nutmeg
¼ teaspoon ground ginger
¼ teaspoon ground cloves

GRAHAM CRACKER CRUST

2 cups graham cracker crumbs
20 vanilla wafer crumbs
¼ cup granulated sugar
¾ cup (1 ½ sticks) unsalted butter, melted

Preheat the oven to 350 degrees F.

CHEESECAKE In the bowl of a stand mixer, or in a large bowl using an electric hand mixer, combine the cream cheese and sugar. Add the eggs, one at a time, and mix well. Add the sour cream, pumpkin, cream, vanilla, cinnamon, nutmeg, ginger, and cloves; mix thoroughly to incorporate, scraping the bottom and sides of the bowl with a rubber spatula.

GRAHAM CRACKER CRUST In a small bowl, combine the graham cracker crumbs, vanilla wafer crumbs, sugar, and butter. Pat the crumb mixture into the bottom of 9-inch springform pan. Pour the cheesecake mixture into the pan and bake for 1 hour.

After 1 hour, turn off the oven. Leave the cheesecake in the oven for 2 hours, making certain not to open the oven during this time. Remove the cheesecake from the oven and remove the outside of the pan. Refrigerate until ready to serve.

SOUTHERN-FRIED APPLE HAND PIES

» MAKES 10 TO 12 HAND PIES

These hand pies have been taste tested by the most opinionated Southern gentlemen I know. Bob Keen Sr., who owns the barn where I board my horse, said that the only other person who could make a good pie like this was his mama. For him, the pies brought back childhood memories of his mama standing over the stove in the farmhouse that still stands on their ranch. These pies can be prepped the night before frying for a hot, fresh breakfast treat.

- 10 to 12 large baking apples (such as Granny Smith, Macoun, McIntosh, or Braeburn)
- 4 tablespoons unsalted butter
- 3 tablespoons brown sugar
- 1/4 to 1/2 cup granulated sugar
- 1 tablespoon cornstarch
- 1/2 cup water, hot
- 1 teaspoon ground cinnamon
- 1/4 teaspoon ground nutmeg
- Homemade pie crust (page 107) or biscuit dough (page 144)
- Canola oil, for frying
- Granulated or powdered sugar, for dusting

Peel, core, and chop the apples into small pieces. Melt the butter in a 10- to 12-inch skillet. Cook the apples over medium heat for 15–20 minutes, until soft. Sprinkle with brown sugar and granulated sugar, adjusting for sweetness, while they cook. Stir occasionally with a wooden spoon, making sure the apples don't stick or burn. When the apples are nearly done, dissolve the cornstarch in water and add to the apples; continue cooking to thicken the juice. Remove from heat, add the cinnamon and nutmeg, and stir to combine. Let the pie filling cool completely. You can prep the apple filling a day or two ahead and refrigerate until you assemble the pies.

Line a half sheet pan with parchment paper and set aside.

On a lightly floured surface, divide the pie crust into 4- to 6-inch ovals about 1/8 to 1/4 inch thick. Scoop about 1 tablespoon of the cooled pie filling into the center of each round. Fold over and lightly press down on the filling and the edges. Trim the edges of the hand pie with a small pizza cutter, if necessary, to even out the edges. Crimp the edges of the dough with a floured fork. Place uncooked pies on the parchment-lined sheet pan. (If prepping the pies the night before serving, cover loosely with plastic wrap and refrigerate. Proceed with frying instructions when ready to cook.)

Line another half sheet pan with several layers of paper towels and set aside.

Fill a large, deep skillet with 2 to 3 inches of canola oil. Heat the oil to about 375 degrees F. Place only a few hand pies in the hot oil at a time, so as not to overcrowd the pan or let the oil cool. Fry until pies are brown on both sides, 3–4 minutes. Remove from the hot oil and let drain on paper towels. Sprinkle pies with granulated sugar or dust with powdered sugar while still warm. These are best served warm.

APPLE BRIOCHE STICKY BUNS

»» MAKES 18 TO 20 BRIOCHE BUNS

This brioche dough isn't just for sticky buns. It can be rolled out, cut into strips, and filled with chocolate pieces or raspberry filling for breakfast pastries. Or it can be rolled out, sprinkled with cinnamon and raisins, and then shaped into loaves of bread. Prepare the buns the night before and bake in the morning to serve warm.

APPLE FILLING

3 cups baking apples, peeled and chopped

2 tablespoons freshly squeezed lemon juice

1 teaspoon ground cinnamon

¼ cup granulated sugar

CINNAMON-SUGAR FILLING

2 cups firmly packed brown sugar

1 cup (2 sticks) melted butter

2 teaspoons cinnamon

BRIOCHE

6 cups all-purpose flour

½ cup granulated sugar

1 ½ tablespoons active dry yeast

1 teaspoon kosher salt

5 large eggs, room temperature

1 ¼ cups whole milk, warm (about 115 degrees F)

1 cup (2 sticks) unsalted butter, slightly softened, cut into pieces

CARAMEL SAUCE

1 cup (2 sticks) unsalted butter

2 cups firmly packed brown sugar

1 cup corn syrup

1 (14-ounce) can sweetened condensed milk

1 teaspoon pure vanilla extract

APPLE FILLING Place all the ingredients in a medium bowl. Stir to evenly coat the apples. Set aside.

CINNAMON-SUGAR FILLING Add all the ingredients to a medium bowl and mix to combine. Set aside.

BRIOCHE Mix together the flour, sugar, yeast, and salt in the bowl of a stand mixer. Add the eggs and the milk. Scrape the sides and bottom of the bowl with a rubber spatula to thoroughly combine the ingredients. Change the attachment to the dough hook and mix for about 2 minutes. With the mixer on medium speed, add ½ cup (1 stick) of the butter. Scrape down the bowl and dough hook with the spatula. Continue to mix for about 4 minutes, until the butter is incorporated. Add the remaining ½ cup (1 stick) butter and continue to mix for about another 4 minutes. Scrape the bowl and dough hook again. Continue mixing until the dough is smooth, shiny, and soft, about another 4 minutes. The dough may look sticky and loose at this point, but resist the urge to add more flour, or your brioche may become tough.

Turn the dough out onto a lightly floured surface and knead a few times by hand to form a ball. Butter the mixing bowl and place the dough back in the bowl. Cover loosely with plastic wrap. Let the dough rise until doubled, about 1 hour. Turn the dough out onto a lightly floured surface and knead by hand a few times. Place the dough back in the mixing bowl with the smooth side up, cover loosely with plastic wrap, and let rise until doubled in size, about 1 hour. Meanwhile, make the Carmel Sauce.

CARAMEL SAUCE Melt the butter, brown sugar, and corn syrup in a medium saucepan over medium heat. Once melted, add the condensed milk. Stir occasionally with a wooden spoon to keep the mixture from burning. Cook for about 10 minutes, just until it comes to a boil. While the caramel cooks, prepare two 9 x 13-inch pans or five 9-inch round cake pans by brushing them with softened butter. Set aside. Remove caramel from heat and stir in the vanilla. Pour just enough caramel sauce into each pan to cover the bottom.

Cut the dough in half. Place half the dough back in the bowl and cover loosely with plastic wrap. Place the other half of the dough on a lightly floured surface. With a wooden rolling pin, roll the dough out into a rectangle shape, about 12 x 18 inches and 1/4 to 1/2 inch thick. Spread half of the Cinnamon-Sugar Filling on the dough. Sprinkle half of the Apple Filling evenly over the dough. Roll the dough up from long side. Cut into about 2-inch pieces and place in the prepared pans, leaving enough space between each roll for them to rise. Repeat the process with the remaining half of the dough. Cover the pans with plastic wrap and refrigerate overnight.

About 1–2 hours before baking, let the buns rise on the counter. Meanwhile, preheat the oven to 375 degrees F. Bake the sticky buns for 30–35 minutes. Remove from oven and immediately invert onto a serving plate. Let cool for a few minutes and serve warm.

CHOCOLATE CHIP NUT COOKIES

MAKES 36 COOKIES

These gooey sweet-and-salty cookies will leave you wanting another bite. The simple, old-fashioned goodness of creamy butter and mixed nuts create a delightful cookie that's best enjoyed with a glass of ice-cold milk.

- 1 cup (2 sticks) unsalted butter, softened
- 1 cup granulated sugar
- 1 1/2 cups firmly packed brown sugar
- 2 teaspoons pure vanilla extract
- 2 large eggs
- 1 cup old-fashioned rolled oats
- 2 1/2 cups all-purpose flour
- 1 teaspoon kosher salt
- 1 teaspoon baking soda
- 1 1/2 teaspoons baking powder
- 1 cup finely chopped nuts (such as walnuts or pecans)
- 1 1/2 cups semisweet chocolate chips

Preheat the oven to 375 degrees F. Line 3 half sheet pans with parchment paper and set aside.

In the bowl of a stand mixer, or in a large bowl using an electric hand mixer, cream together the butter, granulated sugar, and brown sugar. Add the vanilla and eggs. Blend together well. Add the rolled oats, flour, salt, baking soda, and baking powder and combine. Mix in the nuts and chocolate chips.

Scoop cookie dough by the tablespoonful onto the parchment-lined sheet pans, with about 4 rows of 3 cookies each. Bake for 14 minutes, or until lightly golden brown. Let cool slightly on the pans before transferring to cooling racks to cool completely.

PUMPKIN SPICE WAFFLES

» SERVES 4 TO 6

Pumpkin adds moist texture and autumnal flavor to these spiced waffles. Beaten egg whites folded into the batter make these waffles fluffy.

4 large eggs, separated

½ teaspoon cream of tarter

2 ½ cups all-purpose flour

½ cup granulated sugar

1 teaspoon kosher salt

2 teaspoons baking powder

2 teaspoons ground cinnamon, plus more for serving

1 teaspoon ground nutmeg

¼ teaspoon ground cloves

1 teaspoon pure vanilla extract

6 tablespoons unsalted butter, melted

1 cup pumpkin purée

2 cups buttermilk

Pure maple syrup, for serving

Whipped cream, for serving

In the bowl of a stand mixer, or in a large bowl using an electric hand mixer, whip the egg whites with the cream of tartar until fluffy. Set aside.

In a large bowl, combine the flour, sugar, salt, baking powder, cinnamon, nutmeg, and cloves. Add the egg yolks, vanilla, butter, pumpkin, and buttermilk; mix until thoroughly combined. Gently fold in the beaten egg whites with a rubber spatula or wooden spoon.

Preheat the oven to 200 degrees F.

Cook the batter in your waffle iron according to the manufacturer's instructions. Put the waffles in a baking dish and keep warm in the oven while you cook the rest. Serve warm with maple syrup, whipped cream, and a sprinkle of ground cinnamon.

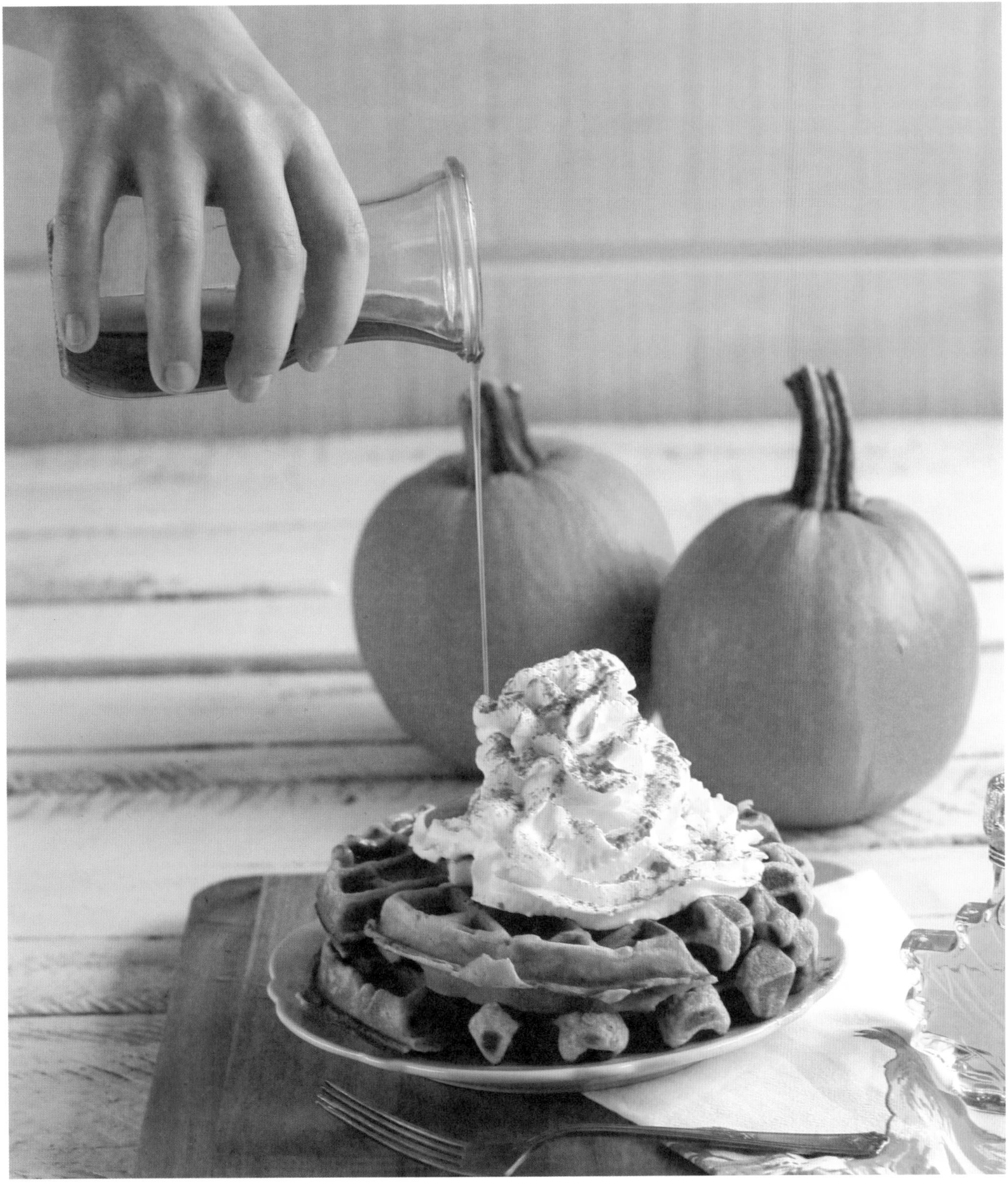

INDEX

D

E

F

G

H

J

L

M

Q

R

S

T

METRIC CONVERSION CHART

VOLUME MEASUREMENTS

U.S.	Metric
1 teaspoon	5 ml
1 tablespoon	15 ml
1/4 cup	60 ml
1/3 cup	75 ml
1/2 cup	125 ml
2/3 cup	150 ml
3/4 cup	175 ml
1 cup	250 ml

WEIGHT MEASUREMENTS

U.S.	Metric
1/2 ounce	15 g
1 ounce	30 g
3 ounces	90 g
4 ounces	115 g
8 ounces	225 g
12 ounces	350 g
1 pound	450 g
21/4 pounds	1 kg

TEMPERATURE CONVERSION

Fahrenheit	Celsius
250	120
300	150
325	160
350	180
375	190
400	200
425	220
450	230

Author of *The New England Farmgirl,* Jessica Robinson grew up on a small Connecticut farm where her family raised livestock and grew crops, as well as operated a maple sugarhouse. Today, Jessica lives on a small farm in Graham, North Carolina, with her husband and two sons. She edits, develops recipes, and provides photographs for her popular blog, *Carolina Farmhouse Kitchen*.

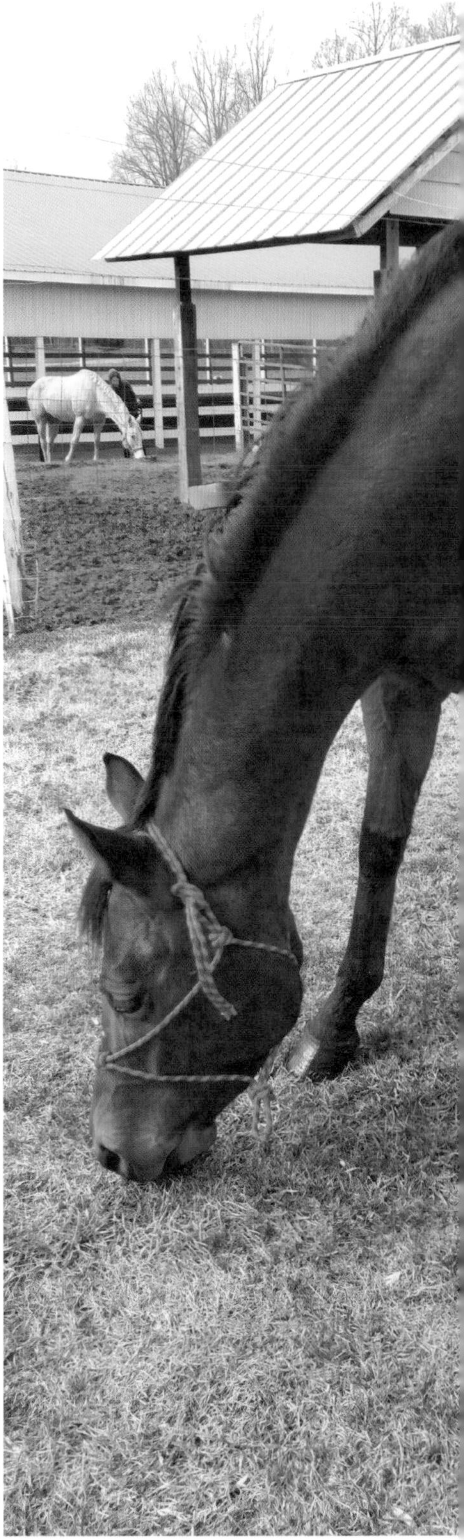